Take Any Book

Hundreds of Activities to Develop Basic Learning Skills Using Any Book

by Neil Stitt

Fearon Teacher Aids

A Division of Frank Schaffer Publications, Inc.

Senior Editor: Kristin Eclov
Editor: Lisa Trumbauer
Cover and Interior Design and Illustration: Rose Sheifer—Graphic Productions

© Fearon Teacher Aids
A Division of Frank Schaffer Publications, Inc.
23740 Hawthorne Boulevard
Torrance, CA 90505-5927

FE7961
ISBN 1-56417-995-8

Table of Contents

Introduction

Dear Teacher,

As in most classrooms, your bookshelves are probably overflowing with books. Most likely, you read the books with your class, or encourage children to practice their reading skills by enjoying the books on their own. After all, what else is there to do with a book?

Plenty! That's the idea behind *Take Any Book*. The activities have been developed to enable you, the teacher, to incorporate any book the class is currently reading into your language arts program, providing opportunities for children to practice essential skills in the Kindergarten–Grade 6 curriculum. The activities allow you to be creative as you adapt them for the level of your students. And best of all, you don't need to buy additional worksheets or reading texts. You can simply choose a book the class enjoys, turn to the chapter in *Take Any Book* that covers the skill you wish to practice, and select and modify the activity that best suits the needs of your students.

The book has been divided into six sections. The first section helps emergent readers recognize letters, both through print and sound. The sections that follow focus on children's ever-developing language arts skills, such as understanding the parts of speech, learning vocabulary words, building words and sentences, and, of course, reading and writing skills. The last section suggests quick activities that require little preparation to review skills and culminate lessons.

The activities in this book serve another purpose as well. They can be used with *all* children, whether they are proficient learners or require a bit of extra attention. The activities are especially helpful to children for whom English is a second language. By allowing children to complete activities orally, with word cards or drawings, children's developmental needs are met and skills reinforced.

Above all, the book invites students to participate in language arts activities as they read books they enjoy. Reading is, after all, a learning as well as an exciting experience.

Happy reading and learning!

Neil Stitt

4

PART ONE

Beginning Word Skills

CHAPTER ONE

Initial Consonants

Recognizing initial consonant sounds is one of the first skills most readers learn. Associating those orals sounds with the actual printed or written letter is a large, but important, step for most young readers. The following activities suggest ways for early readers to listen for and recognize initial consonants, through sound and print, as they explore books on their own.

Activity 1: Create a Consonant Game Board

1 Choose an initial consonant sound to be the focus of the game. Flip through the book children are reading, and select a consonant that occurs often. You might choose a consonant that is of particular difficulty to students.

2 Reproduce and pass out a game board to each student (page 138). Also draw the game board on the chalkboard, large enough for children to write in.

3 Read the book with the class. When children hear the initial consonant, invite them to raise their hands. Pause in your reading, and let a volunteer write the word in a square on the chalkboard while the rest of the class writes the word on their game boards. Explain that they can write their words in any order.

Activity 2: Play Consonant Bingo

1   Have children use their consonant game boards to play Bingo. Use small scraps of construction paper as markers.

2   Invite one child to be the Bingo caller and to come to the board. Ask the child to call out words, erasing them from the chalkboard squares. The rest of the class should place a marker on the word.

3   When students have three markers in a row, either across, down, or diagonally, they call out, "Bingo!"

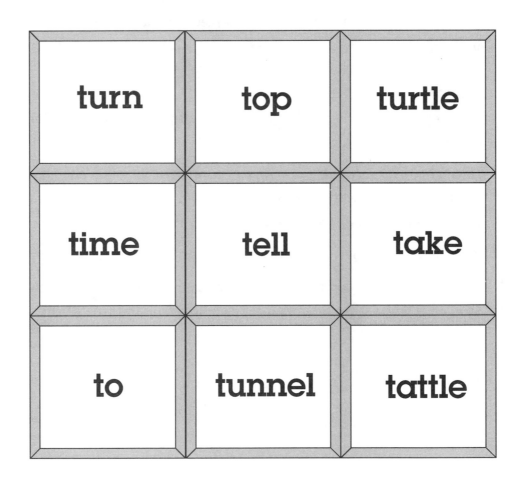

turn	top	turtle
time	tell	take
to	tunnel	tattle

Activity 3: Caterpillar Game

Preparation:

1 Ahead of time, create a caterpillar from construction paper. You will need to cut out 26 circles of about the same size and one circle a bit larger. This will be the head.

2 Slightly overlap the circles and glue them together.

3 Draw a face on the caterpillar head. In each of the remaining circles, write the letters, from A to Z, including the vowels.

4 Set up the caterpillar on a long table or on the floor, along with a game die. You will also need a playing piece for each child participating in the game.

Instructions:

1 Show children the caterpillar, pointing to letters at random for children to identify.

2 Have children place their playing pieces on the caterpillar's head, then roll the die to see who goes first. (The player with the highest number starts the game, then the next highest, and so on.)

3 Tell children to move that number of spaces across the caterpillar.

4 Challenge them to come up with words that start with the letter they land on. They will get one point for each word, up to three words:

1 word = 1 point

2 words = 2 points

3 words = 3 points

5 Monitor children's play to help keep score and to make sure they correctly identify initial letters and words. You might write down children's words to review after the game.

6 The game ends when children roll the die and move off the caterpillar.

7 Review children's words and tally up the scores. The player with the highest score is the winner.

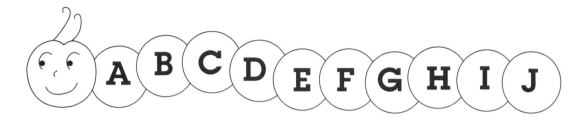

Activity 4: Picture Sounds

1 Choose an illustration from a book children are currently reading.

2 Select an initial consonant that children need to practice and for which many examples can be found in the illustration.

3 Challenge children to find all the objects in the illustration that have that initial consonant sound.

4 As an added challenge, set a time limit. How many objects can children identify in, say, one minute?

Activity 5: Letter Search

1 Working with a small group or an individual, encourage children to find specific letters in books they are reading.

2 Select a page or a paragraph, depending on the level of difficulty. Choose a particular letter, for example, *capital B* or *lowercase p,* challenging children to point to the letter each time it appears.

3 As an alternate activity, choose a sentence or a paragraph from a book students are currently reading or that you have read to them. Write the sentence or paragraph on the chalkboard. Invite volunteers to the board to circle the letters you ask them to identify.

4 Have children copy the words that start with circled letters in their writing journals to reinforce letter shapes.

Activity 6: Word Box

1 A Word Box encourages children to compare words that have similar initial consonant sounds. Ahead of time, choose a sentence from a book the class is reading.

2 Draw a Word Box, like the one shown below. Write the words in the boxes that have the same initial consonant sounds as the words in the sentence.

3 Write the sentence under the Word Box.

4 Have children choose a word from the Word Box, then find a word in the sentence with the same initial consonant sound. Ask them to underline the word and write it in the appropriate Word Box.

pat park	cold cat	hot had	good gave	time to
bad book	fat fun	lost liked	milk mom	zoo zippers

<u>Mom</u> and I <u>had</u> <u>fun</u> at the <u>park</u>.

She <u>gave</u> me a pretty <u>book</u> <u>to</u> read about a <u>cat</u> that <u>liked</u> <u>zippers</u>.

Activity 7: Alphabet Lottery

1   Ahead of time, create a set of word cards. You will need 21 cards, one card for each consonant. For example, *bear, cake, dog, fan,* and so on. Write the words on the cards, or draw pictures of the words, depending on the level of your class. If possible, select words that are featured in the book children are reading. Place all the cards in a box.

2   Invite children to go through their books to choose the longest words they can find. The books need not be the same. In order to play several rounds of the game, encourage children to choose up to eight words.

3   Then begin to pull cards from the box. Show children each card, encouraging them to read the word on their own, listening for the initial consonant sound.

4   Instruct children to find that same letter in their word, and cross it out.

5   The first player who crosses out all of his or her letters is the winner.

6   Invite the winner to the box to choose the word cards for the next round of play.

7   Continue to play as long as interest holds.

Activity 8: Consonant Concentration

1 Ahead of time, go through a book that children are reading, and write down pairs of words with initial consonants for children to practice.

2 Create a set of cards using these words to play the game *Concentration*. For example, if children are practicing the letter *S,* and in the book there is a picture of a sail and a sun, write each word on a card.

3 Place the cards face down.

4 Turn two cards over at a time. Have children say each word, pointing to the beginning consonant. Do the letters sound the same? Do they look the same?

5 If the two cards are a match, remove them from the table. The player then gets another turn.

6 If the cards are not a match, the player must turn them over again. It is then the next player's turn.

7 Encourage children to take turns turning over two cards at a time, saying the words, and determining if the initial consonant sounds match. Play continues until all the cards have been removed.

8 The player with the most cards is the winner.

CHAPTER TWO

Vowels

Vowels, of course, are also an essential part of learning to read. Children hear vowel sounds all the time. As with consonants, learning to associate the oral sounds with the printed word is a crucial step. Many of the vowel activities here have been adapted from the consonant activities. Apply only those that are suitable to the level of your class.

Activity 1: Create a Vowel Game Board

1 Choose a vowel sound as the focus of the game. Flip through a book children are reading, and select a vowel sound that occurs often. You might choose a vowel that is of particular difficulty to students. Vowel sounds can be short vowels (cat, cup, lip) or long vowels (cake, bike, feel).

2 Reproduce and pass out a game board to each student (page 138). Also draw the game board on the chalkboard, large enough for children to write in.

3 Read the book with the class. When children hear the vowel sound, invite them to raise their hands. Pause in your reading, and let a volunteer write the word in a square on the chalkboard while the rest of the class writes the word on their game boards. Explain that they can write their words in any order.

Activity 2: Play Vowel Bingo

1 Have children use their vowel game boards to play Bingo. Use small scraps of construction paper as markers.

2 Invite one child to be the Bingo caller and to come to the chalkboard. Ask the child to call out words, erasing them from the chalkboard squares. The rest of the class should place a marker on the word.

3 When students have three markers in a row, either across, down, or diagonally, they call out, "Bingo!"

Activity 3: Change-a-Word

1 Write a common phoneme on the chalkboard, for example, -at. On separate index cards, write the consonants, along with blends, such as br-, ch-, pl-, and so on.

2 Pass out the cards to the class. Explain to children that they will make new words with the letters you hand them. Point out that not all the letters will create words.

3 Invite each child to come to the board, place the card in front of the phoneme, and say the word. Challenge the class to determine if it is a real word.

4 Write the true words on the chalkboard to review after everyone has presented their letters.

Activity 4: Vowel Kite Wall Display

1 Ahead of time, create a large diamond-shaped kite from construction paper. Cut out smaller diamonds to serve as the tail of the kite.

2 Choose a word from the book children are reading or that you are reading to them that focuses on a vowel sound they are learning. Write the word on the kite, and tape the kite to a wall.

3 Attach a length of yarn to the kite, then pass out the small diamonds to the class.

4 Have children say the kite word with you. Can they think of other words with this same vowel sound? Help children write their words in the diamonds. You might suggest that children look through their books for words, too.

5 Staple children's diamonds along the yarn to finish the kite's tail.

Activity 5: Picture Sounds

1 Choose an illustration from a book children are currently reading.

2 Select a vowel sound that children need to practice and for which many examples can be found in the illustration.

3 Challenge children to find all the objects in the illustration that have that vowel sound.

4 As an added challenge, set a time limit. How many objects can children identify in, say, one minute?

Activity 6: Letter Search

1 Working with a small group or an individual, encourage children to find specific vowel sounds in books they are reading.

2 Select a page or a paragraph, depending on the level of difficulty. Choose a particular vowel sound, such as short *i* or long *o*, and challenge children to find and say words with that sound.

3 As an alternate activity, choose a sentence or a paragraph from a book students are currently reading or that you have read to them. Write the sentence or paragraph on the chalkboard. Invite volunteers to the board to circle the vowels you ask them to identify.

4 Have children copy the words with the circled vowels in their writing journals to reinforce letter shapes.

Activity 7: Word Box

1 A Word Box encourages children to compare words that have similar vowel sounds and spellings. Ahead of time, choose a sentence from a book the class is reading.

2 Draw a Word Box (see page 10). Write words in the boxes that have the same vowel sounds as words in the sentence.

3 Write the sentence under the Word Box.

4 Have children choose a word from the Word Box, then find a word in the sentence with the same vowel sound. Ask them to underline the word and write it in the appropriate Word Box.

Activity 8: Vowel Chart

1 Set up a chart on poster or mural paper. For column headings, write vowel sounds and one-word examples.

2 Each time children read a book, choose a vowel sound to focus on. Invite children to find all the words in the book with that sound.

3 Invite children to write the words in the appropriate column on the vowel chart.

4 Keep the vowel chart on the wall for children to add to as they read other books.

short a cat	long a bake	short i sit	long i kite
bat	rake	fit	right
back	gate	pig	night
hat	pale	big	bike
sat	sail	wig	Mike
tab	fail	miss	white
nap	make	kitten	
trap			
lag			

Activity 9: Long-Vowel Trees

1 Long vowels can have several spellings. As you read with the class, find examples to share with them.

2 For example, if you read a sentence like, *What do you see across the sea?*, point out that *ee* and *ea* create the same long *e* sound.

3 Have children record these words on a long-vowel tree. Draw the outline of a tree on mural paper.

4 Write the vowel sound on the tree's trunk.

5 On each branch, write a spelling variation of that vowel sound. For example, *ee* and *ea*.

6 On construction-paper leaves, invite children to write examples of words with these spellings.

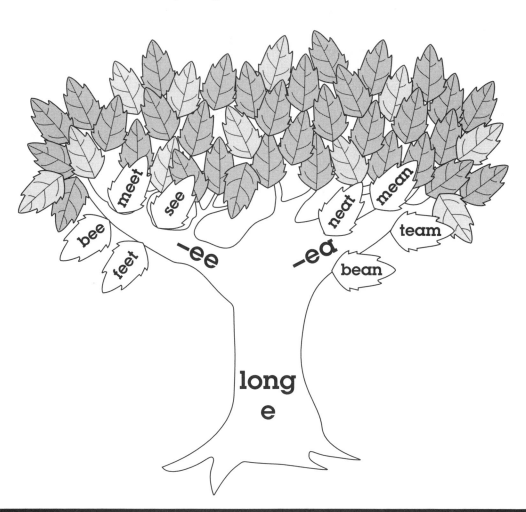

Activity 10: Vowel Concentration

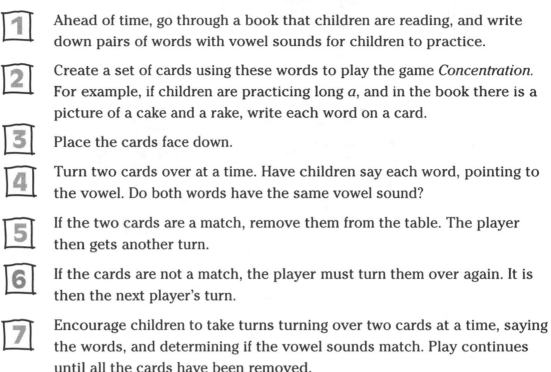

1 Ahead of time, go through a book that children are reading, and write down pairs of words with vowel sounds for children to practice.

2 Create a set of cards using these words to play the game *Concentration*. For example, if children are practicing long *a*, and in the book there is a picture of a cake and a rake, write each word on a card.

3 Place the cards face down.

4 Turn two cards over at a time. Have children say each word, pointing to the vowel. Do both words have the same vowel sound?

5 If the two cards are a match, remove them from the table. The player then gets another turn.

6 If the cards are not a match, the player must turn them over again. It is then the next player's turn.

7 Encourage children to take turns turning over two cards at a time, saying the words, and determining if the vowel sounds match. Play continues until all the cards have been removed.

8 The player with the most cards is the winner.

CHAPTER THREE

Rhyming Words

One of the first types of literature children probably responded to was nursery rhymes. Therefore, children respond naturally to rhyming words. They enjoy the way they sound and can often memorize and recite them. Exploring words that rhyme not only helps with auditory discrimination, but with letter and sound recognition, too.

Activity 1: Getting Familiar with Rhymes

1 Select several nursery rhymes or other poems in children's anthologies. You might choose poems that reflect the current time of year or a particular theme you are exploring.

2 Write the poems on poster paper, then read them with the class.

3 Talk with children about what makes poems special. Help them notice the rhyming words, perhaps highlighting them with a yellow marker. Have children say the words with you to hear the similar sounds.

Activity 2: Rhyme Search

1 Once children understand and are comfortable with the concept of words that rhyme, invite them to come up with rhyming words for books they are reading.

2 Help children choose several simple words from their books. Write the words on chart paper, or have children write the words in their writing journals.

3 Challenge children to supply words that rhyme with their book words. For example, if a child chooses the word *ball,* have him or her write words such as *hall, wall, fall,* and *call.*

4 As you read other books with the class, pause every so often, choose a word, and challenge children to offer words that rhyme with it.

Activity 3: Write-a-Rhyme

1 As children look through their books to find words that rhyme, or as they come up with rhyming words for words in their books, invite them to write short poems with them.

2 Here is an example from *The Bravest Dog Ever: The True Story of Balto* by Natalie Standiford.

Gunnar, Gunnar, it is bright.
You can see the stars at night.

3 Have children write their rhymes on drawing paper, then illustrate them. Display the rhymes with copies of the book in your reading center.

Activity 4: Find-a-Rhyme

1 Look through a book that children are currently reading. Select several words, then come up with rhyming words for them. For example, if you choose the word *ship,* a rhyming word might be *chip.*

2 Present children with rhyming words written on index cards. Place the cards in a box, and have children pick a card.

3 Challenge children to look through their books to find rhyming words such as *pig, fish, cat, bear, snake, deer,* or *fox.*

Activity 5: Picture Sounds Game

1 This game works best in small groups. Choose an illustration in a book children are currently reading.

2 Say a word that rhymes with an object in the illustration. For example, if a cat is in the picture, you might say the word *mat*.

3 Challenge children to find the item in the picture that rhymes with the word.

4 Continue until you've exhausted all possibilities.

Activity 6: Rhyme Riddles

1 Invite children to work with partners. Make sure each child has a copy of the same book.

2 Have partners ask each other riddles. The object to discover the rhyming word.

3 For example, one partner might say, "I am looking at page eight. I see a word that rhymes with *bike*. It is someone's name. What is it?"

4 The other student must identify the rhyming word, then it is his or her turn. Rhyming clues can also be in the illustrations: "I am looking at the picture on page 10. I see an animal that rhymes with *box*. What is it?"

Activity 7: Rhyme Chart

1 Set up a chart on poster or mural paper. For column headings, write the word you would like children to rhyme.

2 Encourage children to look through books they are reading to find words that rhyme with the words on the chart.

3 Invite children to write the words in the proper columns.

4 Keep the rhyme chart on your wall for children to add to as they read other books or to help children as they write rhymes of their own. See the rhyme chart on page 23 for suggestions.

cat	feet	night	dark
bat	meet	right	shark
fat	beat	kite	park
at	wheat	light	bark
chat	seat	bite	
pat			
hat			

Activity 8: Rhyming-Word Concentration

1 Ahead of time, go through a book that children are reading, and write down pairs of rhyming words. Or, choose words from the book that you wish children to learn, and pair each with a rhyming word.

2 Create a set of cards using these words to play the game *Concentration*. Matching cards will be rhyming words. For example, rhyming pairs might be, cake/bake, bat/cat, run/fun, Jack/back, and so on. Write each word on a card, or draw a picture of it.

3 Place the cards face down.

4 Turn two cards over at a time. Have children say each word out loud. Do the words rhyme?

5 If the two words rhyme, or are a "match," remove them from the table. The player then gets another turn.

6 If the cards are not a match, the player must turn them over again. It is then the next player's turn.

7 Encourage children to take turns turning over two cards at a time, saying the words, and determining if they rhyme. Play continues until all the cards have been removed.

8 The player with the most cards is the winner.

CHAPTER FOUR

Syllables

Some words have one syllable, like *dog*. Some words have two syllables, like *doughnut*. And some words have many syllables, like *dictionary*. The ability to hear individual syllables in a word is important for reading, writing, and listening. The following activities help children understand the concept of syllables as they hone auditory discrimination and listening skills.

Activity 1: Listening to Syllables

1 On separate sheets of paper, have children write the numbers *1, 2,* and *3.*

2 Go through a book you are reading with the class, and clearly pronounce some of the words.

3 Have children listen closely to the word. How many syllables do they hear? Ask students to hold up the paper with the correct number.

4 Review children's answers to make sure everyone has correctly counted and understands what syllables are.

Activity 2: Syllable Clap Along

1 Point to pictures in a book you are reading with the class.

2 Have children identify the picture.

3 Ask them to say the word again, this time clapping with each syllable.

Activity 3: Syllable Chart

1 Set up a chart like the one below.

2 As you explore a book with the class, invite children to sort the words by writing them in the proper columns.

3 Review the words in each column by asking children to either clap the syllables or to hold up their papers with the numbers *1, 2,* or *3.*

1 syllable	2 syllables	3 syllables
dog	hello	cabinet
box	table	afternoon
rock	pencil	syllable
chair	paper	eleven

Activity 4: Syllable Game

1 Create four to six game boards, using the pattern on page 138. In each square, glue a picture of an easily identifiable object. Ideally, pictures should be related to any books you are currently reading in class.

2 You will also need to create a spinner. You might use one from a game you have in class, or construct the spinner on page 144.

3 Working with a small group, pass out one card to each child. Review the words on the card.

4 Then spin the spinner. (You might let children take turns.) Have children look for words with that number of syllables. For example, if the spinner stops on 2, children might have the word *cookie* or *flower* on their cards. Ask children to place a paper marker on a square with a two syllable word in it. Mark only one word at a time, even though there might be several words with that number of syllables.

5 The first player to cover up all the squares on the game board is the winner.

Activity 5: Syllable Game, Advanced Version

1 This game is just like the one described in Activity 4, only this time children are using more squares and words from their books.

2 Reproduce and pass out the game board on page 139.

3 Encourage children to flip through their books. In each square on the game board, have them write one word from the story.

4 Then follow the directions in the Syllable Game on page 25.

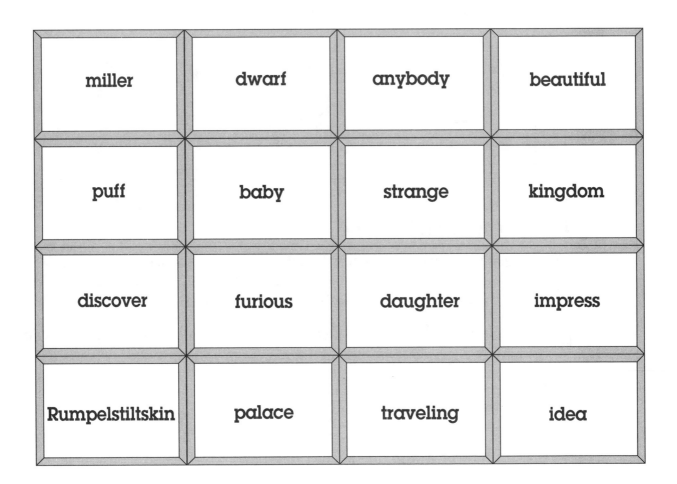

miller	dwarf	anybody	beautiful
puff	baby	strange	kingdom
discover	furious	daughter	impress
Rumpelstiltskin	palace	traveling	idea

PART TWO

Parts of Speech

Chapter 5: Nouns

Chapter 6: Verbs

Chapter 7: Adjectives

Chapter 8: Prepositions

CHAPTER FIVE

Nouns

Nouns, along with verbs, are the backbone of any sentence. Be sure to review with children that nouns are words for objects. They can be people, places, and, of course, things. They can be the subject or the object of a sentence. Help children recognize nouns as they participate in the following activities.

Activity 1: Picture Nouns

1 Invite children to flip through a book they are reading and study the illustrations. What objects do they see?

2 Work with children to identify all the objects as you write them down.

3 When all possibilities have been exhausted, review children's words. Make sure they understand that these are words for people, places, or things.

Activity 2: Noun Search

1 Invite children to study the words in their books. Can they identify the nouns?

2 Write one of the sentences on the chalkboard. Point to various words, asking children if they are nouns. You might ask, "Is it a person? Is it a place? Is it a thing?"

3 Record the words on a separate sheet of paper for children to review. Make sure they understand why each word is a noun.

Activity 3: Noun Visuals

1 Invite children to flip through magazines to find pictures of objects. Have children cut out the pictures and glue them to construction paper.

2 Ask them to write the word for each picture on an index card. If possible, suggest they use words from books they've read.

3 Place the pictures on a chalkboard ledge or on the floor. Collect all the cards into a pile.

4 Divide the class into groups. Give a group the cards, and challenge them to match the nouns with the correct pictures. Time how long it takes.

5 Invite another group to try, timing them as well. Continue until all children have had a chance. The group with the best time wins.

flowers   cup

Activity 4: Noun Sort

1 Place three boxes on a table. Label one box *person,* another box *place,* and the last box *thing.*

2 One by one, hold up the picture cards from the previous activity. Ask children to identify each as a person, place, or thing, reminding them that these are nouns. Place the cards in the correct boxes.

3 Leave the cards and boxes in your learning center. Challenge children to sort the cards on their own.

Activity 5: Noun Chart

1 Start a three-column chart on poster paper. Label one column *Person,* the middle column *Place,* and the third column *Thing.*

2 Choose a book children are currently reading, and invite them to help you find all the nouns. Depending on the level of the book, you might choose to work with only several pages at a time.

3 As children call out a noun, ask them if it is a person, place, or thing. Invite them to write the noun in the correct column of the chart.

4 Make sure children understand that names are also nouns. They are called proper nouns. Have children write names in the appropriate column, too.

Person	Place	Thing
wizard	forest	tree
boy	lake	stone
woman	castle	ring
Mark		cloud
Merlin		

Activity 6: Noun Search-and-Sort Game

1 On index cards, write the words children suggested from the previous activity. Create another three-column chart, but keep this one blank.

2 Divide the class into groups, and give one of them the cards. Explain that the object of this game is to sort the cards by person, place, or thing as quickly as possible. Time the group.

3 Check the group's work to make sure all the nouns have been sorted correctly.

4 Then invite a second group to try it. The winning team is the group that has the most correct answers in the shortest amount of time.

Activity 7: Which Is a Noun?

1 On strips of paper, have children write their favorite sentences from a book they are reading.

2 Demonstrate how to cut the strips to separate the words. Place all the words in a box.

3 Invite children to pick a word, read it to the class, then tell if it is a noun. Ask the rest of the class to confirm the answer.

4 If the word is a noun, it is the next player's turn. If the word is not a noun, the student must pick another word until a noun is found.

5 Continue until all students have had a chance to identify a noun.

Activity 8: Noun Bingo

1 Invite children to play a game of Bingo, choosing words from a book they are reading. Reproduce and pass out Bingo game boards. Depending on the level of your students and the books they are reading, you might choose a nine-, sixteen-, or twenty-five-square game board from pages 138–140.

2 Encourage children to go through the book to search for nouns. Have them write a noun in each square of their game boards.

3 When the game boards are complete, go through the book yourself to call out nouns. Record the words you call out on the chalkboard.

4 Instruct children to place a paper marker on each word they hear.

5 The player who has markers running in a straight line across, down, or diagonally is the winner and shouts, "Bingo!"

CHAPTER SIX

Verbs

Verbs are action words. Verbs come in many forms and many tenses. For example, children might not realize that the word *is* is a verb, because no action is actually taking place. The word *sit* is also a verb, and so are its tenses, such as *sitting* and *sat.* The following games and activities have been designed to help strengthen children's understanding of verbs, tying verbs to the books they read.

Activity 1: Verb Search

1 The best way to start focusing on verbs is for children to search through books they are reading to identify them. In their writing journals, invite children to jot down all the verbs they see. Or, as a group activity, have children suggest verbs as you write them on chart paper.

2 Talk with children about the verbs. Ask guiding questions such as, "What is the action? Who is doing the action? Can you think of another word that means the same thing?"

3 Keep your verb list posted in the classroom for children to refer to as they try some of the following activities.

Activity 2: Verb Visuals

1 Invite children to flip through magazines to find pictures of people doing things. Have children cut out the pictures and glue them to construction paper.

2 On an index card, encourage children to write the verb that best describes the action. If possible, suggest that they use words from books they are reading.

3 Place the pictures on a chalkboard ledge or on the floor. Collect all the cards into a pile.

4 Give a group the cards, and challenge them to match the verb with the correct picture. Time how long it takes.

5 Invite another group to try, timing them as well. Continue until all students have had a chance to play. The group with the best time wins.

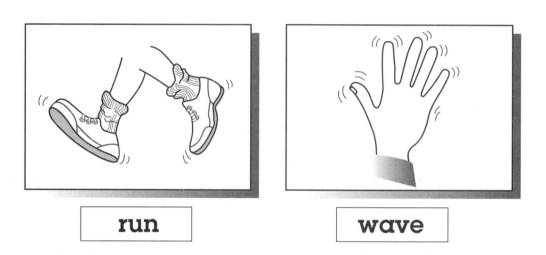

run   wave

Activity 3: Who, What, When, Where, Why

1 Invite children to select sentences they enjoy from books they are reading. Have children write their sentences on index cards, then share them with the class.

2 In most books, sentences are written in the past tense. For example, the sentence isn't, *Abbey watches the waves from the window.* It's *Abbey watched the waves from the window.* Write the present and past tenses on the chalkboard for children to notice the differences.

3 Collect children's cards and mix them up. Then invite one student to select a card and read it to the class.

4 Talk about the contents of the sentence by asking questions. For example, for the sentence, *Abbey watched the waves from the window*, you might ask:

- Who is the sentence about?
- What is she doing?
- Where is she?
- When might she be doing this?
- How would you describe the waves?
- Why is she watching the waves?

Questions will vary according to children's proficiency.

Activity 4: Story News

1 Invite children to talk about stories they read as if they are conducting a news broadcast.

2 Have a student sit behind your desk or at a table, pretending it is the news desk. Give him or her a microphone or an object representing a microphone.

3 Challenge each child to tell about the story in a short news broadcast. Encourage him or her to use as many verbs as possible.

4 Discuss the news report by asking the rest of the class who, what, when, where, how, and why questions. Explain that these are the questions reporters try to answer as they tell us the news.

Activity 5: During the Day

1 Reproduce the clock pattern on page 143. Give one pattern to each student.

2 Help children put the clock together by cutting out the pieces and attaching the hands in the middle with a brad.

3 Tell children a time. Have them move the clock hands to show the time. Ask children what they do at this time.

4 Encourage them to answer using only a verb. For example, if the time indicated was lunchtime, they should say, "Ate."

5 Have children provide an entire sentence using the verb. For example, "I ate lunch."

Activity 6: Tic-Tac-Toe with Verbs

1   Draw a large tic-tac-toe grid on the chalkboard.

2   Divide the class into two teams, designating one as the Xs and the other as the Os.

3   Say a word, and challenge a team to come up with the past tense. If they are correct, they can mark a place on the tic-tac-toe grid. If not, it is the other team's turn.

4   The winner is the team that places its Xs or Os in a straight line, across, down, or diagonally.

Activity 7: Questions and Verbs *Is, Are, Do, Does, Can*

1   This game is a wonderful diagnostic tool for oral language and comprehension. Write each of these verbs on an index card: *is, are, do, does,* and *can.*

2   Pass out blank index cards, and have children draw a picture that represents something in a book they are reading.

3   Place the picture cards in one pile, and the verb cards in another, face down. Also set up a bowl with about 50 playing chips or markers.

4   Taking turns, have children pick a card from each pile. The object of the activity is to create a question, using the verb on the card, that asks something about the picture.

5   If the player has correctly formed the question, he or she gets a playing chip. The game ends with the first player to reach a set number of chips.

6   Encourage more advanced students to write out their questions. Remind students to use question marks.

Activity 8: Is, Are, Was, Were

Working in teams, invite children to play these games using the verbs *is, are, was,* and *were.*

Game 1: Divide the class into two teams. Explain that Team A is responsible for the words *is* and *are,* and Team B is responsible for the words *was* and *were.* Set a timer. Have both teams search for their words in a book the class is reading, and then write down the sentences in which the words occur. After the buzzer rings, invite the teams to share their sentences.

Game 2: Divide the class into two teams. Assign words to each team. Set the timer, and invite the first team to write a sentence that tells about a book they are reading, using the word *is* or *are.* The second team writes a sentence using the word *was* or *were.* Teams get a point each time they say a sentence before the buzzer goes off. The first team to read a set number of sentences is the winner.

Game 3: Use picture cards or illustrations from a book children are reading. Divide the class into two teams, assign each team the verbs *is* and *are* or *was* and *were.* Show each group a picture, and invite the group to write sentences about it using their verbs.

CHAPTER SEVEN

Adjectives

Children use adjectives all the time, and they probably don't even realize it. When they say they had a "great time" at a party and they ate "chocolate ice cream," they are using adjectives. Adjectives are words that describe things. Often adjectives answer the question, "What kind?" For example, what kind of party was it? A great one! What kind of ice cream did you have? Chocolate!

Activity 1: Adjective Chants

1 Encourage children to recite these chants to become familiar with adjectives and how they are used. Ask children to think of an item they have at home. Is it old or new? What color is it?

2 Invite children to share their items. Write each child's name, item, old or new, and color on the chalkboard.

3 Then recite the following chant:

Calvin has a bike. An old green bike.
Oh, how he likes his old green bike.

Rosa has a sweater. A new pink sweater.
Oh, how she likes her new pink sweater.

4 Invite students to the chalkboard to underline the adjectives in each chant.

5 Have the class recite the entire chant together. You might have each student recite the first line of his or her chant, with the class chiming in on the second line.

Activity 2: Memory Game

1 Show children an illustration from a book the class is reading, or display a picture that relates to the book.

2 Allow children to study the picture for about 30 seconds to memorize the details.

3 Then cover up the picture. Challenge children to recall as many details as they can about the picture. Make sure each response includes an adjective. For example, if a student says the picture had a ball, ask, "What color was the ball?"

4 Record children's ideas.

5 Then show the picture again to check children's answers.

Activity 3: Guess the Illustration

1 Using a book that children are reading, invite each child to choose an illustration.

2 Challenge students to write a few sentences about the illustration, using as many adjectives as possible.

3 Invite children to take turns reading their descriptions to the class.

4 After each reading, challenge the class to figure out which picture has been described.

5 Encourage children to compare paragraphs that describe the same illustration. Which adjectives were the same?

Activity 4: Adjectives as Clues

1 Working with partners, invite children to go through their books to find a mystery object they would like their partners to guess.

2 Have children write down three phrases that describe it, then present the phrases to their partners. Make sure children include adjectives.

3 After the first clue, challenge partners to guess the object. Continue until partners correctly identify the object.

4 An example might be: *Hard shell; green body; short legs. What am I? A turtle!*

Activity 5: Let's Pair Up

1 Ahead of time, select 10-16 nouns from a book your class is reading. You should have one noun for every two students. For example, if 28 students are in your class, choose 14 nouns.

2 Write each noun on an index card. Make a second set of index cards using the same nouns.

3 Place one set of cards in a bag, and place the second set in a separate bag.

4 Divide the class in half. Ask each child from the first team to pick a card from the first bag, while students from the other team select cards from the second bag.

5 Invite each member of one team to come up with three adjectives that describe the noun on his or her card.

6 Challenge each member of the other team to figure out if the adjectives describe the noun on his or her card. Remind children that a noun can be a person, place, or thing.

7 When a student believes the noun to be a match, check both the cards.

8 The game continues until all the pairs have been found.

9 If you have other nouns from the story, let children play the game again, this time switching roles.

Activity 6: Adjective Scavenger Hunt

1 Ahead of time, choose nouns from a book that are accompanied by adjectives. Write the nouns on the chalkboard.

2 Encourage children to read the book, looking for the nouns and adjectives that describe them. Have children write down their adjectives, nouns, and the page numbers on which they are found.

3 For children who are reading longer books, provide them with the page number along with the noun. Challenge them to focus their reading on the noun and its adjectives.

CHAPTER EIGHT

Prepositions

Prepositions are often considered spatial words. They tell us the relationship between nouns, verbs, and sometimes adjectives. For example, in the sentence *The bird is in the tree,* the word *in* is the preposition. It tells us the relationship between the bird, the tree, and the verb *is.* Below is a list of common prepositions.

aboard	before	except	on	under
about	behind	for	onto	until
above	below	from	out	up
across	beneath	in	outside	upon
after	beside	inside	over	with
against	between	into	past	within
along	beyond	like	since	without
among	by	near	through	
around	down	of	to	
at	during	off	toward	

Points to keep in mind when practicing prepositions:

- Prepositions can often be confusing for children for whom English is not the primary language. The words can have a variety of meanings and usages and may not directly translate to the prepositions in children's primary languages.
- Prepositions are often combined with verbs to form expressions that might be difficult to comprehend. For example, the phrase "to fly off the handle" means to get angry.
- Oral practice with pictures and actions that illustrate prepositions are essential for comprehension of prepositional concepts.

Activity 1: The Preposition *In*

1 Gather a variety of objects that can fit in a box or container, such as pencils, erasers, toy cars, small balls, crayons, plastic animals, and math manipulatives. You might choose objects that relate to a book the class is reading.

2 Invite a student to choose one object and place it in the box, while saying, "The eraser is in the box."

3 Continue with the remaining objects.

Activity 2: The Preposition *At*

1 Display pictures of places, such as a beach, the zoo, a doctor's office, a restaurant, or an ice-cream parlor, that relate to a book the class is reading.

2 Have children identify the place, then use it in a sentence with the word *at*. For example, "I saw a lion at the zoo."

3 Ask children "where" questions pertaining to the pictures, such as "Where is the lion?" (At the zoo.) "Where are the children?" (At school.)

4 Point out to children that the preposition *at* helps tell us where.

Activity 3: Prepositions from a Bag

1 Go through a book the class is reading to find prepositions. Write them on index cards.

2 Place the cards in a bag or other container.

3 Invite children to take turns choosing a card.

4 Challenge children to use the word from the card in a sentence that pertains to the book. Have younger children say the sentence. Encourage older children to write the sentence.

5 Go over the sentence with the class, pointing out the preposition to make sure it is used correctly.

6 Invite children to illustrate their sentences or find pictures in the book that match their sentences.

Activity 4: Preposition Drawings

1 Supply children with drawing paper and crayons or colored markers.

2 Explain to the class that they are going to follow your directions to draw a scene related to a book the class is reading.

3 Select a place from the book as a central frame of reference, such as a house, boat, tree, or lake. Ask children to draw it.

4 Then provide children with directions, like those below. Ask children to listen closely to the directions, drawing the figures accordingly.

On the right side, draw a _____ .

On the left side, draw a _____ .

At the top draw, a _____ .

At the bottom, draw a _____ .

Draw a _____ inside the _____ .

Draw a _____ outside the _____ .

Draw a _____ in front of the _____ .

Draw a _____ below the _____ .

Draw a _____ above the _____ .

5 Invite children to compare their pictures, checking to make sure each item is placed correctly. Encourage them to appreciate their classmates' interpretation of the scene.

Activity 5: Book Sentences

1 Choose 10 sentences from a book children are reading that contain prepositional phrases, and write them on the chalkboard.

2 Invite children to copy the sentences, underlining the prepositions.

3 Have children draw pictures to illustrate the sentences.

4 Encourage students to come up with additional sentences using the same prepositions.

5 For an added challenge, ask children to write sentences that contain a chain of prepositional phrases, for example, *The cat ran across the street, through the flower garden, around the barn, down the path, and up a tree.*

Activity 6: Prepositional Search and Find

1 Choose three prepositions that occur in a book children are reading.

2 Review the prepositions by inviting children to demonstrate them. For example, if the preposition is the word *on,* ask children to sit on the floor.

3 Help children fold a sheet of paper into three parts.

4 Then instruct children to look through the book to find an example of the preposition, either in the illustrations or the text.

5 Depending on the level of your students, invite children to draw a picture to illustrate the preposition or to write the sentence as it appears in the book.

Activity 7: Prepositional Hide-and-Seek

1 Choose an object that represents something in a story the class is reading. Show the object to the class.

2 Choose a team of about three to four players, and invite them to step outside the room for a moment.

3 Hide the object.

4 Invite the group back in the room. Provide directions with prepositional phrases to help the group find the object. For example, "It is under a book. It is between two shelves. It is near the fish tank."

5 Switch groups as interest holds.

Activity 8: Prepositional Pictures

1 Challenge children to find an illustration in a book as you provide hints using prepositional phrases.

2 For example, "I see a child on a bike. I see a bee inside a flower. I see a cat sleeping under a bush."

3 Reverse the procedure, encouraging children to provide prepositional clues for you to locate the picture.

4 Expand the activity to include pictures from magazines or other books.

PART THREE

Listening to Words

CHAPTER NINE

Synonyms

Synonyms are words that have the same or similar meanings. Studying and recognizing synonyms is an ideal way to not only build vocabulary, but also to enhance reading comprehension.

Activity 1: Understanding Synonyms

1 Write this sentence on the chalkboard, and read it to the class: *At the zoo, I saw a large elephant.*

2 Point to the word *large*. Explain that it is an adjective.

3 Ask children to think of other words that mean *large*. Start a list of synonyms that students know.

4 Record children's words in a word web. Write the sentence in the center circle of the web, underlining the synonym. In the surrounding circles, write words that have the same or similar meaning.

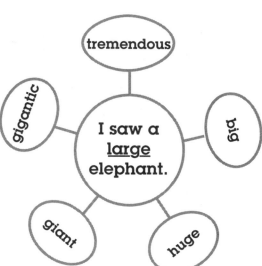

Activity 2: Synonym Story Search

1 With the class, go through a book children are reading, and select sentences that children like. Write the sentence on the chalkboard.

2 Erase one of the words, challenging children to replace it with a new word that means the same thing.

3 For example, the sentence might read, *Jack gave Mary a bouquet of beautiful flowers.* Erase the word *beautiful,* and challenge children to come up with a similar word, such as *pretty, lovely, good-looking, gorgeous, magnificent,* or *handsome.*

4 Be sure to choose not only adjectives, but nouns, as well. For example, in the sentence above, challenge children to come up with another word for *flowers,* such as *blossoms* and *blooms.*

Activity 3: Verbs as Synonyms

1 Write the word *walk* on the chalkboard. Invite a child to the front of the room to demonstrate the action taking place.

2 Then ask children which other words could describe the action of someone walking. Invite children to look through dictionaries and thesauruses and jot down their ideas.

3 Invite children to share their *walk* synonyms with the class. Words children might suggest include *saunter, stroll, march, step, plod, trudge, stride, strut,* and *shuffle.*

4 For each word, ask a volunteer to demonstrate the motion.

5 Continue with other words selected from children's reading.

Activity 4: Synonym Socks

1 Invite children to look through books they are reading to find pairs of synonyms. Ask children to write them down. Depending on the level of your students, you might wish to do this yourself ahead of time.

2 Pass out cutouts of two socks to each student. Instruct them to write a synonym on each sock.

3 Mix up the sock cutouts in a laundry basket. Working in groups, invite students to rummage through the socks to find the matching pairs of synonyms.

Activity 5: Synonym Speed Game

1 Divide the class into two teams.

2 Invite the first member from each team to the front of the room. Write a word on the chalkboard, or say it aloud.

3 Challenge children to think of a synonym and say it as quickly as possible.

4 For each correct answer, the team gets one point. If the answer is incorrect, even if it was the quickest answer, the team loses a point.

5 Encourage children to check any discrepancies in a dictionary or thesaurus.

6 Once each child has had a turn, continue playing as interest holds.

7 To make the game more meaningful, use words that have some significance to books children are reading.

Activity 6: Build a Synonym House

1 Help children create a house shape from a 10" x 13" (25 cm x 35 cm) sheet of manila paper. See example below.

2 In the pointed top, write a book title.

3 In each portion, write a word found in the book.

4 Challenge children to build the house by writing synonyms on scraps of construction paper and taping them next to the appropriate word on the house. The words can be those found in the book or ones children know.

5 Review the words to make sure they are correct.

6 Display children's synonym houses in your reading or language arts center.

CHAPTER TEN

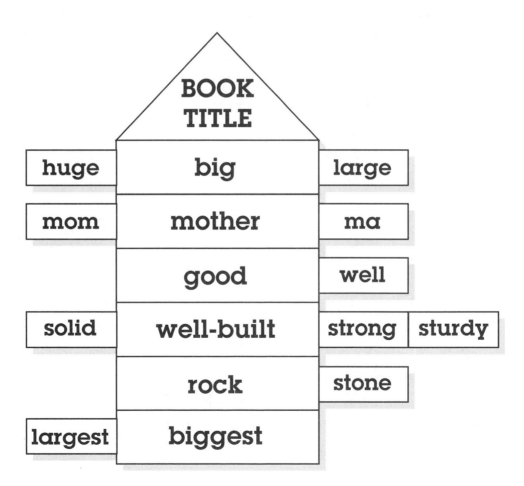

Antonyms

Antonyms are words that mean the opposite of each other, for example, *big* and *small.* As with synonyms, studying and identifying antonyms is a wonderful way to build vocabulary, stimulate interest in language, and sharpen reading comprehension. Below is a list of common antonyms to help with the activities that follow. Invite children to look for these antonyms in stories they read.

no/yes	difficult/easy	night/day
in/out	winter/summer	cloudy/sunny
more/less	hard/soft	black/white
on/off	over/under	curly/straight
his/her	stand/sit	square/circle
up/down	asleep/awake	win/lose
hot/cold	laugh/cry	tight/loose
all/none	happy/sad	thick/thin
high/low	different/same	hello/good-bye
good/bad	begin/end	good morning/ good night
big/small	below/above	man/woman
pretty/ugly	right/wrong	boy/girl
short/tall	right/left	walk/run
open/close	before/after	

Activity 1: Antonym Concentration

1 Challenge children to choose words from books they are reading, then come up with antonyms for them. (You might do this ahead of time, depending on the level of your students.)

2 Have children write each word on an index card.

3 Instruct children to combine their cards with a partner's.

4 Tell students to place all the cards face down on a table.

5 Have them follow the rules for Concentration, turning over two cards at a time to find a matching pair. In this case, the pair is a set of antonyms, such as *on/off* or *up/down*.

6 The player with the most pairs wins.

Activity 2: Antonym "Go Fish"

1 Have partners or groups of four combine the word cards they used for Antonym Concentration.

2 Ask them to shuffle the cards and pass out four to each player. Have them place the rest of the cards in a pile, face down.

3 The object of the game is to collect as many matching pairs of antonyms as possible. The first student asks a player if he or she has the antonym to a card in his or her hand. For example, "Do you have the opposite of *cold?*"

4 If the player does, he or she must hand it over. The other player removes the cards from her or his hand and takes two cards from the pile.

5 If the player does not have the card, the other player takes one card from the pile. If a "match" is made, he or she shows it to the group, removes the pair, selects two more cards from the pile, and goes again.

6 Play continues until all the antonyms have been matched. The player with the most pairs of antonyms is the winner.

Activity 3: Antonym Books

1 Create a class book for children to record pairs of antonyms they discover. Gather about five sheets of drawing paper, and fold them in half. Staple the pages together down the fold.

2 Invite volunteers to decorate the cover of the book.

3 Encourage all children to contribute to the book, writing each word on facing pages. Have them illustrate the pages, too.

4 Create books as needed.

Activity 4: Antonym Bingo

1 Reproduce and pass out a 16-square Bingo grid (see page 139).

2 Have children choose eight pairs of antonyms, writing each word in a square. If possible, ask children to select antonyms found in a book the class is reading.

3 Then call out pairs of antonyms. Have children place a paper marker on each word that is called, covering two words at a time.

4 The first player to cover squares in a straight line, across, down, or diagonally is the winner.

Activity 5: Illustrated Antonym Chart

1 Encourage children to discover antonyms in books they are reading. Set up a chart with a book title written across the top.

2 Each time children discover a new pair of antonyms, encourage them to write the antonyms on the chart. Encourage them to illustrate the antonyms, too.

3 Be sure to review children's word choices.

4 Start a new chart each time the class begins a new book.

Activity 6: Antonym Stories

1 Working with partners, invite children to retell a story they recently read. Have them write simple sentences, underlining words that have antonyms.

2 Invite partners to exchange their stories with another pair of students. Challenge them to rewrite the stories, exchanging the underlined words with antonyms.

3 Have children read their new stories to their classmates.

Activity 7: Antonym Team Game

1 On separate index cards, write words that can be paired with antonyms.

2 Form a circle on the classroom floor or outdoors with a large hoop or length of string. Spread out the cards within the circle.

3 Divide the class into teams. Give each team a beanbag or other small item to toss. Invite them to toss the item so it lands on one of the cards. If the object does not touch a card, it is the next team's turn.

4 Remove the card from the circle and read it to the group, challenging them to provide the antonym.

5 Give each team one point for each correct antonym.

6 The team with the most points wins.

CHAPTER ELEVEN

Homonyms

Homonyms, or homophones, are words that sound the same but have different spellings. Because these spellings can often confuse children, it helps to point out the differences as children learn the meaning of each. Below are some common homonyms children might come across in their reading.

pair/pear	here/hear	we'll/wheel
there/their/they're	plane/plain	ant/aunt
bear/bare	dear/deer	for/four
two/too/to	no/know	eight/ate
see/sea	feat/feet	hour/our
fare/fair	meat/meet	write/right
bee/be	sail/sale	piece/peace
bye/buy	pale/pail	one/won

Activity 1: Homonym Book Search

1 With the class, go through a book children are reading. Point out any homonym pairs in the book.

2 Write the words on the chalkboard. Invite children to write the words in their journals or on a sheet of paper.

3 Discuss the meaning of each word.

4 To reinforce and associate the homonym spellings with their meanings, encourage children to illustrate one of the words in each pair . For example, in the pair *sail/sale,* children could illustrate and label the sail of a boat.

Activity 2: Complete the Sentence

1 Choose words from a book the class is reading that can be paired with a homonym.

2 Write a sentence on the chalkboard, including a pair of homonyms found in the book.

3 Read the sentence with the class. Challenge children to select the correct homonyms. Invite a volunteer to the board to circle them.

Activity 3: Homonym Concentration

1 Select several pairs of homonyms that you are currently reviewing with the class or that relate to a book the class is reading. Write each homonym on a separate index card.

2 Place the cards on a table, face down.

3 Instruct children to turn over two cards at a time to find matching homonyms. Have students continue by following the traditional rules of Concentration.

4 The game ends when all the matches have been found. The player with the most matches wins.

Activity 4: What a Pair!

1 Draw a mitten pattern. Reproduce the pattern so each child has two mittens.

2 Assign a pair of homonyms to each student.

3 Ask them to decide which homonym is most easily illustrated. Invite them to draw a picture of that homonym on one mitten.

4 On the other mitten, have children write the word for the other homonym.

5 Spread the mittens out on a table. Divide the class into groups, and challenge each group to match the homonyms.

6 If appropriate, time the groups. The group who is the quickest to correctly match all the homonyms is the winner.

Activity 5: Homonym Stories

1 Write the homonyms that children have learned on a large sheet of poster paper.

2 Challenge children to use the homonyms in stories of their own. Suggest that the stories relate to a book they are currently reading.

3 Encourage children to exchange their papers with partners to check if they have used the homonyms correctly.

4 Invite children to share their stories with the class.

CHAPTER TWELVE

Idioms, Similes, Metaphors

So many of the phrases incorporated into the English language don't fall into any category. These are phrases we say all the time, that by themselves don't mean anything. But when applied to circumstances or experiences, they take on a whole new dimension. Review some of the sayings below with the class. Then encourage the class to look for these figurative words and phrases as they read.

out of sight	cry over spilled milk	jump out of one's skin
all thumbs	drop in	keep an eye on
at the drop of a hat	early bird gets the worm	keep your shirt on
back-seat driver	falling out	let the cat out of the bag
bed of roses	fed up	raise the roof
beside the point	fits like a glove	snake in the grass

A few points to note about idioms:

- Students who have English as a second language may have a difficult time comprehending and translating figurative words and phrases. Assign a classmate to help explain idiom meanings.

- Sometimes idioms are specific to a region of the country. That could be the case with some of the phrases on this list. Add others to the list that are popular where you live.

Activity 1: Similes

1 Share with children that a simile is way to compare two things using the words like or as. For example, *The students were so active, they were busy as beavers.*

2 Invite children to look through their books to find examples of similes.

3 Point to pictures in the books and start a sentence for children to complete. For example, you might point to an ocean and say, "This ocean is as blue as . . .". Ask children to finish the sentence. For example, "This ocean is as blue as the sky, as a blueberry, as my eyes."

4 Write the similes children discover on chart paper. Make sure children notice the words *like* or *as* in the phrases.

For example:

The pillow was as fluffy <u>as the fur of a kitten.</u>

The setting sun looked <u>like a bright orange lollipop.</u>

Activity 2: Metaphors

1 Share with children that metaphors are similar to similes, except they do not use the words *like* or *as*. These are a bit harder to identify.

2 Have students look through a book the class is reading. Have them select the names of people, places, and things from the book with which they are familiar.

3 Brainstorm with children words that help them describe these images from the story.

4 Then arrange children's ideas into metaphors. Help children understand how metaphors help us describe things.

For example:

My friend is <u>a bright, shining star.</u>

My cat is <u>a big bag of warm fuzzies.</u>

© Fearon Teacher Aids FE7961

PART FOUR

Word Building

CHAPTER THIRTEEN

Compound Words

Classmate. Homework. Bookstore. Say these words to the class. Can children tell what they have in common? They are made by combining two words. Words that are made up of two words are called compound words. Invite children to look through books they are currently reading to find other compound words. Suggest that children record the words in their writing journals. Invite children to explore compound words further with the following activities.

Activity 1: Word Scramble

1 Reproduce the puzzle-piece patterns from page 141, and give several copies to each student.

2 Instruct children to write each word of their compound words in a separate puzzle piece. Then cut them out.

3 Invite children to mix up the pieces, then challenge a classmate to put the compound words back together. Encourage children to share the books where they found their compound words.

Activity 2: Compound Match

1 Ahead of time, write the two words of a compound word in the puzzle pieces on page 141. Cut out the pieces.

2 Pass out the pieces randomly among the class. Ask one student to share the word on his or her puzzle piece.

3 Challenge children to figure out if they have the missing word that will make the compound word complete. Encourage children to put both of their words together.

4 Continue until everyone has found their compound word matches.

Activity 3: Drawing Compound Words

1 Write each of the following compound word parts on separate index cards: *fire, snow, horse, foot, base, boat, meat, ball, house, dog, bird, sail, cake, pan, light, shine, glasses,* and *sun.*

2 Mix up the cards, and spread them out face down on a table.

3 Invite a student to choose two cards. If the student feels the two words make a compound word, let him or her keep the cards. If not, ask the student to choose two more cards.

4 Once children are satisfied with their compound words, invite them to draw pictures of them. Have children label the picture with the compound word.

5 Culminate by inviting students to share their pictures with the class, explaining how the compound word relates to a book the class is reading.

6 Combine children's pictures into a class book of compound words.

Activity 4: Compound Bingo

1 Depending on the level of your students, pass out a nine-, sixteen-, or twenty-five-square Bingo game board found on pages 138-140.

2 Review with children the compound words they have discovered as they read their books.

3 Ask children to write each compound word in a Bingo square in random order.

4 Then invite a student to call out compound words. When children hear their words, have them cover the word with a scrap of construction paper.

5 The object is to cover all the squares in one row, either across, down, or diagonally. The first player to do so calls out, "Bingo!"

Activity 5: Compound Pictures

1 Invite children to work with partners or in small groups to look for pictures that can create compound words. For example, children might find a picture of a sun and a picture of glasses. Putting the pictures together makes the compound word *sunglasses*.

2 Provide children with magazines to cut up. As children flip through the pages, encourage them to be as creative as possible to build compound words. Suggest that they check their words in a dictionary to confirm that they do, indeed, make one word.

3 Spread out poster or mural paper on a table. As children make compound words, have them glue the pictures to the paper, connected by a plus sign. Have them write the compound word underneath.

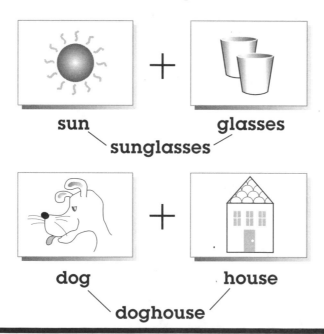

sun + glasses
sunglasses

dog + house
doghouse

Activity 6: Compound Word Chain

1 Write the word *doghouse* on the chalkboard. Then write the word *houseboat*. Point out to children that they could almost connect the two words, creating a word chain: *doghouse-houseboat*.

2 Challenge children to come up with their own word chains of compound words. Mention that it's tricky. They might wish to consult a dictionary to make their chains as long as possible.

3 To get children going, start them off with the word *basketball*. What word might come next? (For example, *basketball-ballpark-parkway-.*)

Activity 7: Good Beginnings and Endings

1 Write the beginning of a compound word on the chalkboard, such as *any*. Challenge children to go through books they are reading to find compound words that begin with this word, in this case, *anyone, anything,* and *anywhere*.

2 Reverse the activity by presenting the ending of a word, such as *man*. Have children find compound words in their books that end with man, such as *policeman, fireman, doorman,* and *mailman*.

CHAPTER FOURTEEN

Prefixes and Suffixes

Prefixes and suffixes are small groupings of letters added to words to make new words. Some common prefixes and suffixes are listed below. Invite children to investigate prefixes and suffixes in the books they read to determine how they affect the meanings of words.

Prefixes	Suffixes
pre-	-ly
un-	-able
under-	-ing
dis-	-ive
tele-	-est
inter-	-al
mono-	-y
re-	-ful

Activity 1: Word Search

1 Encourage children to look through their books to discover words that have prefixes or suffixes. Have them write down their words.

2 Invite children to share their words with the class as you write them on the chalkboard.

3 Help children identify the prefix and the suffix, then explain from which main word, or root word, the word is built.

Activity 2: Prefix and Suffix Chart

1 Reproduce and pass out the cluster chart from page 142.

2 As children review the prefixes and suffixes they discover, have them write each as a column heading on the chart.

3 Encourage children to use their charts to record other words that have these prefixes and suffixes. Suggest that children add new prefixes and suffixes to the chart as they discover them.

Activity 3: Build-a-Word

1 Go over the list of words that contain prefixes and suffixes the class came up with for a book they are reading.

2 On separate index cards, write the suffixes, prefixes, and root words children found. Write each several times, enabling children to create many words.

3 Gather the cards in a box. Let children rummage through the box, choosing prefixes, suffixes, and roots words to build new words.

4 Encourage children to write their new words on separate sheets of paper. Ask them to exchange their papers with classmates to share their words.

5 For further confirmation, suggest that children check their words in a dictionary.

Activity 4: Prefix and Suffix Bingo

1 This variation of Bingo challenges children to use not only listening and reading skills, but also critical thinking skills. Reproduce and pass out a nine-square Bingo game board (page 138).

2 Ask children to look over their prefix and suffix charts or word lists, and write a root word in each Bingo square.

3 Then call out prefixes or suffixes. As children look at the words on their cards, challenge them to consider which word can be made by adding the prefix or suffix to it. If a word can be made, have children cover the square with a scrap of construction paper.

4 For example, if a child has written the word *wonder*, and you have called the suffix *-ful*, he or she can cover a square containing the word *wonderful*. But if you have called the suffix *-ive*, the child cannot cover the word because *wonderive* is not a word.

5 Provide plenty of time between call-outs for children to try out the prefixes and suffixes with their words. They should only cover one word each time.

6 The first child to cover all the squares in one row running across, down, or diagonally is the winner.

Activity 5: Team Game

1 Using the cards you created in the previous activity, encourage children to work in groups to form sentences with words they build.

2 Have the first team build a word and present it to the opposing team, challenging them to include the word in a sentence.

3 The team has the choice of using the word with its prefixes and suffixes or writing a sentence with only the root word. If only the root word is used, the team gets one point. If the team incorporates the word with prefixes or suffixes, the team gets two points.

4 Instruct the groups to take turns, building words and using them in sentences.

5 Set a limit of 10 words. Then have children add up their scores. The team with the most points wins.

Activity 6: Write-a-Word

1 Encourage children to go through their books again to look for words with prefixes and suffixes.

2 Ask children to write the entire sentence from the book.

3 Challenge children to dissect the prefix or suffix word until only the root word remains.

4 Instruct children to write a sentence with the root word.

5 Have children compare the sentences to notice how the new word changes the tone and meaning of the sentence.

6 As a follow-up activity, suggest that children incorporate all the sentences into a new story.

Activity 7: Exploring Prefix Meanings

1 Share with children that prefixes change the meanings of words because they have meanings themselves. With the class, look through a book to find words with prefixes. Challenge children to explain what they think the prefixes mean.

2 Start a list of prefixes and words that start with them. As children study the lists, challenge them to draw conclusions about the meanings of the prefixes.

3 You might prepare several sentences with words that have prefixes, however, leave the prefixes off. Encourage children to read the sentences, adding the prefix to the word so the sentence makes sense.

re- = again	pre- = before	un- = not
reheat	preheat	uncut
review	preview	unselfish
recheck	prewash	unlucky
reteach	precut	unequal

Activity 8: Before and After

1 Challenge children to go through books they have read to find words that have both a prefix and a suffix, such as *unbelievable* or *distasteful*.

2 After children have located ten words, ask them to exchange their papers with a classmate. Invite children to discuss what their words mean.

3 Have children check their words in a dictionary to confirm their meanings.

Activity 9: Prefix and Suffix Grid

1 Pass out index cards, and ask children to write one prefix or suffix they have learned.

2 Arrange the cards on a bulletin board.

3 Ask children to help you connect the cards with strands of yarn, creating an eye-catching grid.

4 Invite children to the bulletin board to point out their prefix or suffix contributions. Have each child then call on a classmate to supply a word with this beginning or ending.

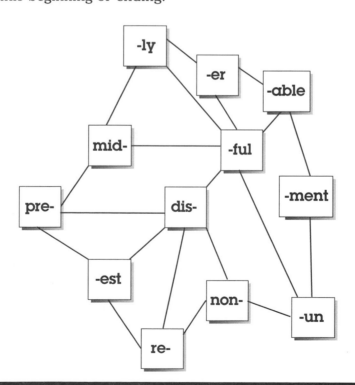

Activity 10: Looking through Magazines and Newspapers

1 Encourage children to expand their prefix and suffix searches to include magazines and newspapers. Provide children with periodicals that they can cut up.

2 When children find appropriate words, ask them to cut out the words and glue them to sheets of art paper to make a collage.

3 Again, talk about the words children discover, helping them notice the prefixes, suffixes, and root words.

Activity 11: Writing with Magazine and Newspaper Words

1 Invite children to pretend they are magazine or newspaper writers.

2 Ask them to write a headline for a story that uses one or more of the words from their prefix-and-suffix collages.

3 Followup by encouraging children to write a few sentences about their headlines.

Activity 12: Prefix and Suffix Concentration

1 Invite children to match words that have the same prefixes and suffixes. Have children first find the words in a book they are reading, or use words from a class chart.

2 Write words with matching prefixes and suffixes on separate index cards.

3 Instruct children to place the cards in rows on a table, face down.

4 Then have children follow the traditional instructions for Concentration. Remind them to turn over only two cards at a time. If the cards have the same prefix or suffix, they can keep the pair and go again. If not, they must turn the cards back over, and it is the next player's turn.

5 The game ends when all the pairs have been found. The player with the most pairs is the winner.

Activity 13: Beat the Clock

1 On separate index cards, write several prefixes and suffixes. Place them in a pile, face down.

2 Working in small groups, reveal the first card and set a timer for, say, two minutes.

3 Challenge children to look through books, magazines, newspapers, and other materials for words with the prefix or suffix.

4 Players get one point for each word they find.

5 After children have searched for five prefixes or suffixes, have them add their points. The team with the most points wins.

CHAPTER FIFTEEN

Root Words

Remind students that we build words by adding letter groupings to them, like prefixes and suffixes. However, the main part of the word is still there. This is called the root word. The following activities focus on root words, which children briefly explored in the previous chapter.

Activity 1: Word Puzzles

1 Invite children to find words in a book they are reading that have prefixes or suffixes. Tell them to write the words on a sheet of paper.

2 Pass out the puzzle pieces from page 141.

3 Instruct children to write the prefix on the first puzzle piece and the root word on the second, or vice versa.

4 Mix up the puzzle pieces. Challenge children to put the words together, noticing how the prefixes and suffixes fit together with the root words.

Activity 2: Root-Word Concentration

1 Choose words from stories children are reading that have prefixes or suffixes. Write the entire word on one card, then write the root word on another card. For example, if the word is *dishonest,* write *dishonest* on one card, and *honest* on the other.

2 Instruct children to arrange the cards in rows, face down.

3 Review with children the directions for Concentration. Explain that in this version, they are to match the entire word with its root word.

4 Remind them that the game ends when all the cards have been removed.

5 The winner is the player with the most matching pairs.

Activity 3: Root-Word Match

1 Share with children that some root words can have both a prefix or a suffix.

2 On separate index cards, write the root word, the root word with the prefix, and the root word with the suffix. Provide several different root words, preferably from a book children are reading.

3 Mix up all the cards.

4 Challenge children to group the cards by finding the common root words.

5 Check children's groupings to make sure they have correctly identified the root words.

Activity 4: Root-Word "Go Fish"

1 Create a set of game cards for children to play a variation of the game *Go Fish*. Select words that can have multiple endings, for example, *jump*, *jumps*, *jumping*, and *jumped*. Write each word on a separate card.

2 Mix up all the cards, and pass out four to each student. The remaining cards are placed face down in a pile in the center of the table. Tell children that the object of the game is to get a complete set of four cards with the same root word.

3 Explain that they are to play this game as they would Go Fish, and review the rules with them.

4 The game ends when all the sets have been found. The player with the most sets is the winner.

CHAPTER SIXTEEN

Contractions

A contraction is a combination of two words by using an apostrophe. Usually part of the second word is missing. For example, in the contraction *wouldn't,* the contraction for *would not,* the *o* in *not* is missing. Contractions shouldn't be confused with possessives, which also use apostrophes. Below are some common contractions children might come across in their reading, along with the words that make them.

I am	I'm	can not	can't
you would	you'd	it is	it's
you are	you're	do not	don't
she is	she's	we have	we've
that is	that's	did not	didn't
let us	let's	they are	they're
are not	aren't	is not	isn't

Activity 1: Contraction Search

1 Write a contraction on the chalkboard to provide children with an example. Dissect the contraction, showing children the two words from which it is made.

2 Challenge children to go through books they are reading to find other contractions and write them down.

3 Ask children to share their contractions with the class.

4 On a sheet of chart or poster paper, start a list of the contractions children find. Keep the list posted, inviting children to add to it as they discover new ones.

Activity 2: Contraction Practice

1 Ahead of time, write the words that form contractions on separate index cards, such as *I, you, he, she, it, we, they, who, that, am, would, will, have, not, would, should, is, there,* and *can.*

2 Spread out the cards on a table.

3 Write a contraction on the chalkboard.

4 Invite a student to the table to find the two words that make up the contraction.

5 Have the student show the cards to the class to confirm the answer.

Activity 3: Contraction Equations

1 Using the word cards from the previous activity, invite children to solve contraction equations.

2 Lay out two cards on a table, connected by a plus sign and followed by an equals signs.

3 Challenge students to figure out the contraction that the two words make, writing the answer on a blank card. Have them place the card after the equals sign.

4 Suggest that children record their contraction equations in their writing journals.

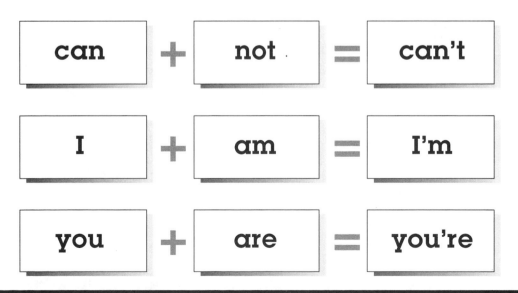

Activity 4: Contraction Game

1 Divide the class into two teams. Set up two "quiz" desks at the front of the room, facing the class, complete with answer cards and markers.

2 Invite two children to sit at the desks with their backs to the chalkboard. Explain that you are going to give them two words from which to make a contraction.

3 Have children write their answers on their cards as you write the answer on the chalkboard.

4 Have children show their cards to the class to match with the answer on the board.

5 Teams get two points for each correct answer.

6 Continue the game until each child has had a turn. Then total up the points. The team with the most points wins.

Activity 5: Contraction Concentration

1 For this version of Concentration, children will be matching contractions that are formed with the same ending word, for example, *can't* and *don't*. Both have the word not as the second word.

2 Write each contraction from the matching pair on an index card. Other matches might include *I'll/you'll, that's/it's, you're/they're, I've/we've,* and *I'd/you'd.* You can use some endings several times, just make sure you have an even number of contractions so children can make a pair.

3 Have children lay the cards face down on a table, then follow the traditional rules of Concentration. The player with the most pairs once all the cards have been removed is the winner.

Activity 6: Contraction Guessing Game

This game invites children to ask each other questions using contractions. It helps build not only listening skills, but also oral language, auditory discrimination, and thinking skills.

1. Ahead of time, collect a variety of small items, such as a ball, a plastic toy, a stuffed animal, and a small book. Place each item in a brown paper lunch bag.

2. Arrange a small group of children into a circle. Ask one student to be "It" and to leave the group for a moment. Then hand out the bags, one for each remaining student.

3. Ask children to look into their bags, remember their objects, close the bags, then place them in the middle of the circle.

4. Invite "It" back to the circle. Have the child choose a bag and take out the object. In order to determine to whom the object belongs, encourage "It" to ask questions using contractions. For example:

   I've found a toy car.
   It's red and blue.
   I don't know who it belongs to.
   Doesn't it belong to you?

5. The child asks the final question to one of the group members. If this was the child's object, that child becomes "It," and the game repeats.

6. If not, the child chosen says, "It couldn't belong to me."

7. "It" continues to ask group members the last question until the owner is found.

8. Vary the contractions according to the level of the group and those children discovered in books they've read.

Activity 7: Contraction Bingo

1 Pass out a 16-square Bingo game card to each student (page 139).

2 Review contractions children found in a book the class is reading. Write the contractions on the chalkboard. Make sure you have at least 16.

3 Instruct children to choose 16 contractions and write them in random order in the squares on their game boards.

4 Let one student be the caller. As he or she selects contractions from the list, have the caller erase them.

5 The rest of the class should cover their words as they are called with markers, chips, or scraps of construction paper.

6 When all the squares in one row, either across, down, or diagonally, have been covered, that player calls out, "Bingo!"

Activity 8: Contraction Chart/Activity Sheet

1 Reproduce and pass out the student activity sheet on page 79.

2 Explain the sheet to the class.

3 Then invite children to use the sheet to record contractions they find, as well as the two words from which they are made.

Contraction Chart

Look at the chart below. In the first column write the contraction. In the second column write the two words that make up the contraction.

Keep the chart in your writing folder. Add to it as you find other contractions.

CONTRACTION	TWO WORDS

    © Fearon Teacher Aids FE7961

PART FIVE

Reading Skills

Chapter 17: Sequencing

Chapter 18: Sorting and Classifying

Chapter 19: Charts and Graphs

Chapter 20: Dictionary Skills

CHAPTER SEVENTEEN

Sequencing

Children put things in sequence the first time they count from one to 10 or say the alphabet. Following a recipe, building a model, even singing a song are all instances when things happen in sequence. The ability to recognize and repeat a sequence is an essential cognitive learning skill. The following activities help children sharpen their sequencing skills. With a bit of tweaking, the activities can be applied to books children are reading.

Activity 1: In Picture-Perfect Order

1 Invite volunteers to create picture cards based on a book the class is currently reading. Explain that the pictures should illustrate different objects from the book, such as people, places, or things.

2 Show the pictures to the class and discuss them.

3 Arrange the pictures in random order along a chalkboard ledge or on the floor. Invite children to study the sequence.

4 Then mix up the cards. Challenge children to place the cards in the original sequence.

5 You might let small groups play this game as teams for further incentive.

Activity 2: Sentence Sequences

1 On strips of paper, ask children to write a sentence from a book they are reading.

2 Invite them to cut the sentences apart into individual words.

3   Have children exchange their cut-up strips with classmates. Challenge them to put the words in correct sequence.

4   As a followup, set up several stations of sentence strips. Invite groups to move from station to station to put the sentences in correct sequence. Time the groups' progress. The team with the quickest time wins.

Activity 3: Walking Sentences

1   Invite the class to select a sentence from a book they are currently reading.

2   Assign children one word from the sentence to write on a large sheet of paper.

3   Invite those children to the front of the room in random order to present their words to the class.

4   Challenge the class to arrange their classmates in order so the sentence reads correctly.

5   Repeat the activity with other sentences from the book until each child has had a chance to be a part of a "walking" sentence.

Activity 4: Dialogue Sequencing

1   Choose a book the class is currently reading that contains a lot of dialogue. Select a passage to which children particularly respond. Write each line of dialogue on a separate index card.

2   Mix up the cards.

3   Challenge children to work with partners to read the lines of dialogue and put them in order.

4   Have children refer to their books to check their answers.

Activity 5: Story Sequence

1 Sequencing activities would not be complete without discussing the chain of events in a story. Talk with children about a story they enjoy, remarking on the order in which things happen.

2 Assign to children important moments in the story. Ask them to draw the scenes and write a brief sentence about them.

3 Mix up the pictures, and display them on a bulletin board or flannel board.

4 Challenge the class to put the pictures in story order.

Activity 6: Alphabet Caterpillars

1 Assign each student a letter of the alphabet. Also give each a paper circle, large enough to write in.

2 Invite children to go through a book they are reading to find a word that starts with the letter you assigned. Ask them to write the word in the circle.

3 As children work, create a caterpillar head, and place it on the far left side of a bulletin board.

4 One by one, invite children to the bulletin board. Have them share their book words with the class, then place their paper circles in the correct alphabetical sequence. Use pushpins to temporarily post children's circles, rearranging them as necessary.

5 When complete, review the sequence of words, pointing out that the words have been arranged in alphabetical order.

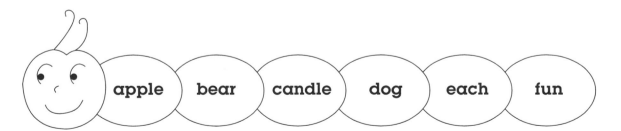

Activity 7: Find-a-Sequence

1 Invite children to think about things that occur in a particular order. For example, the growth of a plant, how cookies are made, how caterpillars change into moths, and even everyday activities such as how we brush our teeth or complete an art project.

2 Have each child choose a sequence. Give each student four index cards.

3 Tell children to illustrate one step of the sequence on each card.

4 Encourage students to exchange their cards with partners, challenging their classmates to place the cards in sequence.

Activity 8: Storybook Time Line

1 Review with children that the purpose of a time line is to organize information in chronological order. Time lines follow the sequence of events.

2 Invite groups to create time lines for stories they read. Roll out a length of mural paper for each group.

3 Tell groups to decide which key moments from their books they would like to show. Ask each group member to take a scene.

4 Instruct group members to draw their scenes on the mural paper, from left to right, in chronological order.

5 Help them draw a line connecting the events to make their story time lines complete.

6 Display the story time lines in your class reading center or in the hallway for others to enjoy.

Activity 9: Recipe Order

1 Reproduce a simple recipe that children can follow along in class.

2 Invite students to help you follow the recipe, pointing out that you must do the steps in order.

3 As children enjoy the food they've made, challenge them to recall the sequence of the recipe. What did they do first? What did they do next? What did they do last?

Activity 10: Comic-Strip Sequences

1 Ahead of time, cut out comic strips appropriate for your class. Glue the comic strips to oaktag to make them sturdy.

2 Cut the comic strips apart, frame by frame.

3 Store each comic strip in its own envelope.

4 Give children the cut-up comic strips. Challenge them to arrange the comic-strip frames in the correct sequence.

Activity 11: Dance Sequence

1 Invite children to share with the class any dance steps they know.

2 Point out that some dance steps follow a particular sequence. Review the individual parts of the dances children share. After you complete one step, ask the class, "What comes next?"

3 Encourage children to teach the dance routine to the class.

4 Then play some music that children enjoy, and invite them to perform the dance steps.

5 Make sure children understand that their movements follow a particular sequence.

Activity 12: Story Starters

1 Invite the class to come up with its own story, pointing out the importance of the sequence of events. Help the class begin by presenting a story starter such as, "One sunny day, something strange happened. First . . . ."

2 Encourage children to provide sentences to tell the story. Suggest that they include such words and phrases as *and then, the next thing I knew, suddenly,* and *finally.*

3 Write children's sentences on sentence strips.

4 Invite the class to place the sentence strips in sequence.

Activity 13: Daily Routines

1 Remind children that our days follow a particular sequence, too. We get up, eat breakfast, go to school or work, come home, and so on.

2 Reproduce and pass out the activity sheet on page 87.

3 Encourage children to record what they do during their days.

4 Help them realize the orderly sequence of daily activities.

Name ______________________ Date ____________

My Day

The things you do every day probably follow a sequence. Record the sequence of your day. Write what you do at each time on the lines below.

7:00 ______________________

7:30 ______________________

8:00 ______________________

8:30 ______________________

9:00 ______________________

9:30 ______________________

10:00 ______________________

10:30 ______________________

11:00 ______________________

11:30 ______________________

12:00 ______________________

12:30 ______________________

1:00 ______________________

1:30 ______________________

2:30 ______________________

3:00 ______________________

4:00 ______________________

5:00 ______________________

6:00 ______________________

7:00 ______________________

8:00 ______________________

CHAPTER EIGHTEEN

Sorting and Classifying

Sorting and classifying are skills children use throughout their lives. These skills rely on the child's ability to compare, contrast, and draw conclusions so they can group like objects. As children sort and classify, they review numbers, words, colors, shapes, and other early learning milestones. Choose the activities in this chapter that meet the needs of your students.

Activity 1: Magazines and Catalogs

1 Arrange the class into groups at individual work tables.

2 Provide the groups with magazines and catalogs that they can cut up.

3 As children flip through the periodicals, encourage them to think of different groupings for the objects they see, such as clothing, household items, plants, animals, places, toys, foods, and so on.

4 Working individually or as a group, invite children to cut out pictures representative of their classifications.

5 Have children make a collage of their cutouts, then challenge their classmates to guess the category.

Activity 2: Classifying Parts of Speech

1 Review with students the parts of speech, such as nouns, verbs, adjectives, and prepositions.

2 Write various words on index cards that represent parts of speech you wish students to practice. Try to choose words from a book the class is reading.

3 Pass out the activity sheet on page 89. Challenge children to sort the words on the cards into the categories on the sheet, writing the words in the proper columns.

Classifying Parts of Speech

Classify words from a story you are reading. Write words from the story in the proper column of the chart below, classifying the words by determining which parts of speech they are.

Nouns	Verbs	Adjectives	Prepositions

Activity 3: Build-a-Word

1 Invite children to review a book they have just read by sorting events and objects by characters.

2 Assign one character from the story to each group of children.

3 Ask groups to talk about their characters and come up with special things about them, for example, something the character did, said, or wore. Have each child in the group write a sentence about the character.

4 Collect all the sentences students have written and place them in a bag.

5 Write the characters' names across a bulletin board.

6 Begin to pull sentences from the bag. As you read each one, challenge children to sort the sentences by characters. To which character does the sentence relate?

7 Tack the sentence beneath the character's name.

Activity 4: Similarities and Differences

1 Invite children to look through their books to find examples of similarities. For example, children might sort objects in illustrations by like colors or shapes. Or note all the objects that were bought at a store. Or find all the objects that are alive. Have children draw pictures of each like object in their category.

2 As children review their items, encourage them to look for differences among them, too.

Activity 5: Alphabet Classification

1 Ahead of time, write the letters of the alphabet on 26 index cards. You might ask a student to help you.

2 Ask children to arrange the cards in alphabetical order.

3 Working in groups, invite students to choose a category such as animals.

4 Instruct children to name an animal. Have them listen to the first letter of the name, then turn over that letter card. That letter can not be used again.

5 The game continues until all the letter cards have been turned over.

6 Invite children to play the game again, this time choosing a new category.

Activity 6: Book Sort

1 For beginning readers, set up letter categories for sorting, such as *S*, *N*, and *P*. Invite students to look through a book they are reading to find words that start with these letters. Have them write the words on cards, then sort the cards into appropriate piles.

<u>S</u>	<u>N</u>	<u>P</u>
so	not	pretty
surprise	next	party

2 For intermediate readers, set up topic categories for sorting, such as foods, sports, and occupations. Invite students to look through a book they are reading to find each item, write it on a card, then sort the cards into appropriate piles.

<u>Foods</u>	<u>Sports</u>	<u>Occupations</u>
hot dog	basketball	teacher
sandwich	uniform	mail carrier

Activity 7: More Ways to Sort and Classify

1 The activity sheets on pages 93, 94, and 95 encourage children to sort and classify the books they read in a variety of ways. Reproduce and pass out the activity sheets as appropriate for your class.

2 "Sort and Classify 1" invites children to classify key elements in the story by people, places, and things.

4 "Sort and Classify 2" encourages children to sort moments in the story.

5 "Sort and Classify 3" asks children to choose a character's name. Demonstrate how to write the character's name in the squares across the top, one letter for each square. (For longer names, have children tape two activity sheets together.) Then challenge children to come up with an object from the story that begins with each letter and fits the categories as designated on the chart.

	D	A	I	S	Y
Places	Dakota	attic	inside		
People	Daisy	Allen			
Foods					
3-syllable Words					
Animals	dog	ant	insect		

Sort and Classify 1

Classify the elements of a book you read into the categories below.

PEOPLE	PLACES
_____	_____
_____	_____
_____	_____
_____	_____
_____	_____
_____	_____
_____	_____

THINGS

_____

_____

_____

_____

_____

_____

_____

Sort and Classify 2

Find words in your story that belong in each category in the chart below. Sort the words by writing them in the box.

animals	
foods	
plants	
toys	
occupations	
weather words	

Reproducible

Sort and Classify 3

Write the name of a story character in the boxes across the top of the chart, one letter per box. Read the categories down the left side. Fill in the boxes with things from the story that begin with each letter.

Character Name					
Places					
People					
Foods					
3-Syllable Words					
Animals					

CHAPTER NINETEEN

Charts and Graphs

Throughout this book, children have been organizing words they learn by recording them in graphs or charts. Mention to children that charts and graphs are important tools for organizing information. The following pages share a few other graphs to experiment with.

Activity 1: Book Bar Graph

1 Explain that a bar graph is a simple way to compare numbers and amounts. Pass out the activity sheet on page 98 for children to follow along with this activity.

2 Suggest to children that they have read a story about a family reunion. How can they easily determine which family brought the most guests?

3 Down the left side of the graph, have children write the names *Uncle Joe, Aunt Bess, Smith,* and *Mary.*

4 Explain that for each family member, children are to draw one person in one box of the chart.

- Only Uncle Joe and his wife came to the reunion.

- Aunt Bess showed up with her two daughters.

- All six members of the Smith family came.

- Mary came with her mother and father.

5 Help children read their charts to determine which family had the most guests.

Joe	☺	☺				
Bess	☺	☺	☺			
Smith	☺	☺	☺	☺	☺	☺
Mary	☺	☺	☺			

Activity 2: Book Pie Graph

1 Reproduce and pass out the activity sheet on page 98. Discuss that a pie graph helps us see the whole picture, providing proportional details.

2 Suggest that children are reading a story about animals in a forest. For example:

- Explain that half the animals are birds. Have children color half the pie graph brown.
- One-quarter of the animals are deer. Have children color one-quarter brown.
- One-eighth of the animals are bears. Have children color one-eighth black.
- One-eighth of the animals are wolves. Have children color one-eighth gray.

3 Help children notice that by "reading" the colors of the graph, we can determine which animal most represented.

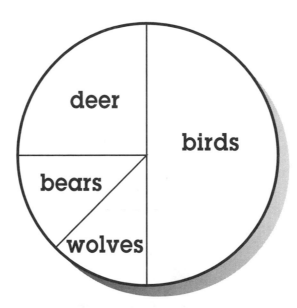

Book Bar Graph

Use this bar graph to count and compare things in stories you read.

Write in the things to be counted.

Draw one item in each box.

Reproducible   © Fearon Teacher Aids FE7961

Book Pie Graph

A pie graph helps us to compare amounts, sizes, and proportions. Use this pie graph to record information about the books you read.

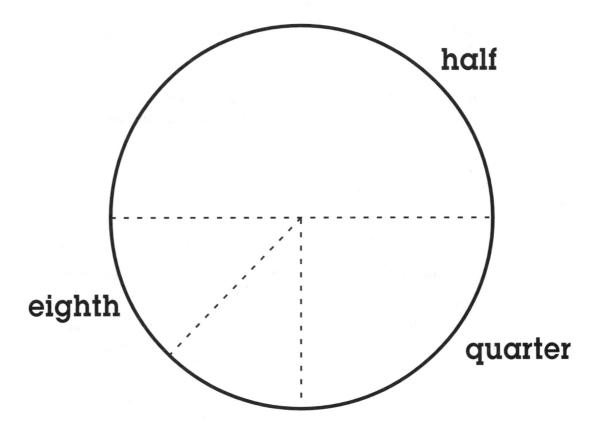

CHAPTER TWENTY

Dictionary Skills

Recognizing letters, reading words, and putting letters in sequence or alphabetical order, are all skills essential to using a dictionary. Encourage children to practice their dictionary skills with these activities.

Activity 1: Dictionary Race

1 Ahead of time, choose 10 words from a story children are reading. Look up the words yourself in a dictionary, and jot down the page numbers.

2 Divide the class into teams, and provide each with a dictionary. Write the 10 story words on the chalkboard.

3 Challenge children to look up the words as quickly as possible and write down the page numbers. Time the groups as they work simultaneously.

4 As children finish, record their times. Check their page numbers to be sure children looked up the words correctly. The team with the quickest time and the most correct page numbers is the winner.

Activity 2: Search and Spell

1 Choose words from the story, and purposely spell them wrong. Write the wrong spellings on the chalkboard.

2 Share with children that dictionaries not only provide word meanings, but also help us to correctly spell words.

3 Have children check the spelling of the words you've written on the chalkboard, looking them up in the dictionary.

4 Encourage children to correct your spelling errors according to the words they find in the dictionary.

Activity 3: Which One Doesn't Belong?

1 Go through a book the class is reading, and select words that children find interesting.

2 Group each story word with three other words—two that have something in common with it and one unrelated word.

3 Write all four words on the chalkboard or on chart paper.

4 Ask children to study the words and figure out which word doesn't belong. Encourage children to consult a dictionary for help.

5 Invite a child to the board to circle the word that doesn't belong. Encourage children to also explain *why* the word doesn't belong.

Activity 4: Story Vocabulary Cards

1 Remind children that when they come across an unfamiliar word in a book they are reading, they can discover its meaning by looking it up in a dictionary.

2 Pass out index cards. Ask children to write a story word on the blank side of the card.

3 Have children look up the word in a dictionary. Tell them to write its definition on the lined side of the card.

4 Point out that children have created vocabulary flash cards. Encourage children to review their cards with partners to enhance their vocabularies and reading comprehension.

Activity 5: Dictionary Concentration

1 Invite children to go through a book they are reading and write down interesting vocabulary words.

2 Pass out index cards. Ask children to write each word on a card, then look the word up in a dictionary and write its meaning on another card.

3 Explain that the word and its meaning form a match.

4 When children have created enough cards, invite them to play a variation of Concentration. Instruct children to arrange the cards in rows, face down.

5 Tell them to take turns turning over two cards at a time. Each time, they must turn over a word and a definition. If they turn over two words or two definitions, they must turn one card back over until they have one word and one definition.

6 Tell children to read the word and the definition out loud. Does the definition define the word on the card? If it does, the player removes the pair from the table and goes again.

7 If not, it is the next player's turn. Play continues until all words have been matched with their definitions. The player with the most pairs wins.

Activity 6: Dictionary Bingo

1 Reproduce and pass out a 25-square Bingo game card from page 140.

2 Go through a book the class is reading, and with students, choose 24 interesting words. Write the words on the chalkboard.

3 Invite children to look up the words in a dictionary, then write the definitions in the Bingo squares in random order. Let children mark the middle square as a "Free Space."

4 Then call out words. Have children search for the word's definition on their game cards and mark it with a chip or scrap of construction paper.

5 The first player to cover all the squares in a row across, down, or diagonally is the winner.

PART SIX

Writing Skills

Chapter 21: Punctuation

Chapter 22: Writing Activities

Chapter 23: Culminating Activities

CHAPTER TWENTY-ONE

Punctuation

When children read, they see all sorts of dots, dashes, and curly shapes. By reading, they probably know these are punctuation marks—those little things that tell us when to pause, ask a question, or get excited. Students need practice with how to use punctuation when they write on their own. The following activities encourage children to sharpen their punctuation skills by discovering the punctuation in books they read.

Activity 1: Finding Punctuation

1 On the chalkboard, write several sentences from a book the class is reading.

2 Read the sentences with the class, guiding children to notice the punctuation marks.

3 Then ask one student to come to the board to circle all the periods.

4 Have another student come to the board to draw a square around all the commas.

5 Ask another student to come to the board to draw a triangle around all the quotation marks.

6 Then review with the class the function of each. Let children practice further by continuing with other sentences from the book.

Activity 2: What's Missing?

1 Again, write sentences on the chalkboard from a book the class is reading. This time, leave out some punctuation, such as a missing period or not capitalizing the first word of the sentence.

2 Read the sentences with the class.

3 Challenge students to identify the errors, and invite them to the board to correct them.

4 You could also have the class work in teams. Ask teams to rewrite the sentences correctly on separate sheets of paper. Encourage the teams to work together to fix the punctuation errors. Review the papers, and score one point for each correct sentence. The team with the most points wins.

Activity 3: Punctuation Partners

1 Assign partners or arrange students into groups. Explain that they are going to help each other practice punctuation skills.

2 Instruct each partner to find several sentences in a book the class is reading that they think would be good for punctuation practice.

3 Have one partner write the sentence, leaving out all the punctuation marks, including capital letters.

4 Tell the other partner to read the sentence and fill in the missing punctuation.

5 Encourage partners to confer, talking about the sentence and then checking it in the book.

6 Invite partners to switch roles.

Activity 4: Who Said It?

1 Remind children that quotation marks alert us that someone is about to speak. The words we read inside quotation marks are words a character is saying.

2 Choose dialogue from a book the class is reading to write on the chalkboard. Then write each book character's name on an index card.

3 Read the sentences with the class. Point out the quotation marks. Explain that all punctuation occurs inside the quotation marks, too.

4 Then invite children to tell you who said each sentence. Place the index cards on the chalk tray, and have children choose a card to tape next to each quote.

5 Discuss children's answers, then encourage them to look through their books for confirmation. As children search for the quotes, once again ask them to notice the use of quotation marks and punctuation.

Activity 5: Question Search

1 Write a question mark on the chalkboard, and ask children to identify it. Talk about how it is used in a sentence.

2 Invite children to look through their books to find sentences that end in question marks. Have children read the sentences to partners.

3 Have children write down their book questions, noticing the question mark at the end of the sentence.

4 As an added challenge, encourage children to answer the questions posed in the book.

Activity 6: Question and Answer

1 Pass out five index cards to each student. Instruct children to write five questions about a book the class is reading, one question per card.

2 Encourage children to exchange their cards with partners.

3 Ask children to read each other's questions, then write the answers on the backs of the cards.

4 Have children share their answers with classmates. Make sure children check their partner's cards for the proper use of punctuation.

Activity 7: Picture Questions

1 Invite children to choose an illustration from a book they are reading and study it for details.

2 Ask children to write five questions about their illustration. Have them leave space below each question for an answer.

3 Have children exchange their papers with partners. Encourage partners to view the illustration and answer the questions.

4 Have partners check each other's work.

5 If students are reading books that do not have illustrations, suggest that they use nonfiction texts related to a theme the class is studying.

Activity 8: Question Conversions

1 Ahead of time, write the questions listed below on separate sheets of paper in black marker:

Where did?   Which should?

What did?   How can?

When could?   Who can?

Why did?   How did?

2 Write any other questions you feel would be appropriate for your class. Display the questions around the room.

3 Read sentences from a book the class enjoys. Write the sentences on the chalkboard.

4 Have children turn each sentence into a question. Encourage them to look at the questions posted around the room to guide them.

5 Invite children to exchange their papers with partners to check to see if they used question marks correctly.

Activity 9: How Exciting!

1 Invite children to find examples in their books of exclamation point usage.

2 By reading several of the sentences aloud, talk about how exclamation points influence sentences. Make sure children realize that this form of punctuation denotes emotion. It can be used when someone is happy, excited, angry, scared, or just trying to make a point.

3 Write this sentence on the chalkboard: *I got a new puppy today.* Read it to the class. Now write the same sentence, only this time with an exclamation point: *I got a new puppy today!* Read the sentence again with feeling.

4 Help children realize how the exclamation point affects the sentence. Have them find sentences with exclamation points in their books and read them out loud. Encourage children to read the sentences with and without feeling. Can they tell the difference?

Activity 10: Punctuate a Picture

1 Choose an illustration from a book the class is reading. Write several sentences about it, but leave out the punctuation, including capital letters.

2 Display the picture for small groups, along with the sentences. Read the sentences with the group. Can they tell what is missing?

3 Encourage children to supply the missing punctuation. Suggest that they refer to the illustration to help with their answers.

4 Depending on the level of your class, have them work in groups, writing sentences to give to another group of classmates.

Activity 11: Something About Commas

1 Encourage children to look through their books to find sentences with commas.

2 Have children choose a sentence that has a lot of commas and write it down.

3 Review children's sentences by writing several on the chalkboard. Read them with the class.

4 While viewing the sentences, speculate with children when they think commas are used.

5 Explain that commas have many uses.

- They separate items in a list, such as apples, bananas, and oranges.

- They appear within quotation marks, such as, "I am going to the store," said John.

- They combine two sentences: *Sue went to school, and her mother went to work.*

Commas, of course, have many uses. These are some basic examples to get children thinking about them.

6 Choose a few more examples from the sentences children provided. Write them on the board without the commas.

7 Invite children to tell you where the commas should go, then ask them to check their answers in their books.

Activity 12: Sentence Structure

1 Go through a book the class is reading, and jot down important nouns, verbs, prepositions, and adjectives.

2 Cut out shapes to represent each part of speech. For example, an apple shape could stand for nouns, a pear could be verbs, a banana could be prepositions, and a strawberry could be adjectives.

3 Write each word in its corresponding shape. For example, each noun will be written in an apple cutout, each verb in a pear cutout, and so on.

4 Invite children to choose shapes and write sentences with them. Have them arrange the shapes into a sentence format, then write down the complete sentence with punctuation, capitalization, articles, and anything else the sentence needs.

5 Have children share their sentences with the class. Ask the class to fix any problems.

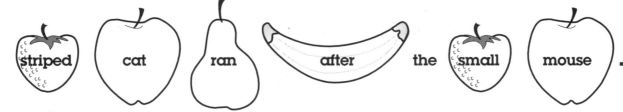

The (striped) cat ran after the (small) mouse .

CHAPTER TWENTY-TWO

Writing Activities

Now it is time to put it all together. Through reading, children have gained an appreciation for language and knowledge about how sentences are formed. Invite them to take what they've learned to write sentences, paragraphs, and even stories of their own.

Activity 1: Write What You See

1 Show the class an illustration from a book they are reading or a picture related to it.

2 Have children write about the picture. Encourage them to describe the scene, including how it relates to the story.

3 Have children exchange their papers with partners to check for spelling, punctuation, and grammar errors.

4 As children view each other's work, encourage them to compare how their classmates' descriptive paragraphs differ from their own.

Activity 2: Remember What You See

1 Try the previous activity again, only this time, encourage children to write from memory.

2 Have them study a picture from a book for about a minute. Encourage them to remember as many details as possible.

3 Remove the picture, and ask children to write about it. Challenge them to use descriptive words to make the picture come to life.

4 Invite volunteers to share their papers with the class. Show the class the picture, and talk about the details the writer included.

Activity 3: What Am I Writing About?

1 Ask children to look around the room and choose an object to describe. Have them write a descriptive paragraph about the object, without telling what the object is.

2 Invite children to read their descriptions to the class.

3 Challenge students to look around the room to figure out the object their classmate is describing.

4 When the object has been correctly identified, talk with the class about the descriptive words that helped identify it.

Activity 4: Who Am I Writing About?

1 Invite children to choose a character from a book the class is currently reading. Or, let them choose a character from a story the class has read in the past or a story that is popular among students.

2 Invite children to write about the character in the first person, without revealing the character's name. For example, *I like to go camping. One time, I had to fight off a bear. Who am I?* The length and complexity of children's work will depend on the level of your class.

3 Ask children to read their descriptions to the class. Challenge students to identify the character.

4 Talk with the class about the words that helped students name the character.

Activity 5: Where Am I Writing About?

1 Describing scenery is another skill-sharpening creative writing activity. Invite students to choose a setting from a book the class has read, or a fictional setting they create themselves, such as a beach, a carnival, or a forest.

2 Ask children to describe the setting, but not reveal what it is.

3 Have children read their descriptions to the class.

4 After each reading, challenge the class to identify the place.

5 Discuss which words and phrases helped children realize the setting.

Activity 6: Book Critique

1 Find books in class with book reviews. You will find these on the back flaps, book jackets, or back covers.

2 Read the reviews with the class.

3 Reproduce and pass out the activity sheet on page 114. Review the questions with the class to make sure children understand them.

4 Encourage children to choose a book and write a review about it, using the activity sheet. Suggest that students use descriptive words and answer the questions in complete sentences.

5 Let children keep all their critiques in a folder. Invite them to review their critiques to remember the books they've read.

Name ________________________________ Date ______________

Book Review

Write about a book you read. Answer the questions below to complete your book review.

My Book Review of

____

(book title)

by

____

(author)

Who were the main characters? ______________________________

____

What did you like about the characters? ____________________

____

What problem were the characters trying to solve? ___________

____

How did they solve the problem? ___________________________

____

How did the story end? _________________________________

____

What were your favorite parts? ___________________________

____

Activity 7: Theme-Based Writing

Preparation:

1 This writing activity requires some preparation on the part of the teacher. Choose a theme the class is currently exploring. It might be seasonal, such as Halloween, Thanksgiving, or the coming of spring. It might be science-related, for example, if your class is studying the ocean, a particular animal, or trees. Or it can be based on a book the class is currently reading.

2 Choose a simple object that is representative of the theme. For example, if the class is studying pond life, you might choose a fish or a turtle. If it is Halloween time, you might choose a pumpkin.

3 Draw the object on a sheet of paper. Reproduce the drawing so you have many copies, preferably on bright paper. Cut out the shapes.

Instructions:

1 With the class, discuss the theme you wish to explore. Brainstorm one-word ideas that reflect the theme. For example, if the theme is Thanksgiving, children's ideas might include a scarecrow, turkey, pumpkin, and so on.

2 Write each word on a cutout.

3 Place the cutouts in a bag. Ask children to each choose one.

4 Tell the child to show the word to the class, then talk about it, describing the object and explaining its significance to the theme.

5 Then display the cutouts around the room. Invite children to use the theme words to write a story. Have children write their stories individually, with a partner, or working in groups.

6 Display children's stories on a bulletin board with an appropriate theme-related title.

7 As an alternate activity, you could have children describe the words on the cutouts, challenging the rest of the class to guess the words.

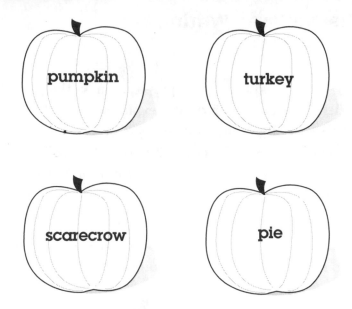

Activity 8: Class Big Book

1 Choose a book the class enjoys or that they are currently reading.

2 Talk with children about parts of the book they enjoy most. Discuss what children like about them, jotting down their ideas.

3 Divide the class into small groups. Assign each group a part of the story to describe and illustrate. Ask children to write a paragraph about this part, describing the action taking place and the characters involved. Have children write a rough draft of their paragraphs to double-check spelling, punctuation, and grammar.

4 Then pass out large drawing paper. As some children in the group rewrite the paragraph, invite others to illustrate the page to depict their scene. Make sure they leave space for the writing paper.

5 Tell children to glue the writing page to the drawing paper.

6 Combine children's papers together in story order to make a class Big Book.

7 Read the Big Book with the class.

Activity 9: Story Frame

1 Another way for children to review a story they have read is to record events and impressions in a story frame. Reproduce and distribute the story frame on page 118.

2 Go over the category in each box with the class.

3 Ask children to choose a book they recently read, and fill out a story frame about it. Encourage children to illustrate their story frames, as well.

4 Suggest that children keep a folder of story frames for all the books they read. This will help them remember the stories and enjoy them again.

Activity 10: Story Sequels

1 Discuss with children the ending of a story they recently read. Speculate what might happen next to the story characters.

2 Working individually, with partners, or in groups, let children write a short sequel to the story. Suggest that they put the story characters in new situations. What would they like to see these characters do?

3 Invite children to share their sequels with the class.

Activity 11: Fill in the Blanks

1 Pass out the Fill in the Blanks activity sheet on page 119. This is a wonderful way to get children who have trouble writing interested in the process.

2 Tell children to complete the story on the page by filling in the blanks. Point out that the word under each line tells them which word they should write, such as a noun, verb, or adjective. You may want to review these parts of speech with the class.

3 Encourage children to read their completed stories out loud. Compare the different words children used, remarking on how the stories differ.

Story Frame

Write about a book you read by answering the questions in the story frame below. Illustrate your answers in each box.

Book Title _____

Author _____

Who is in the story? _____ _____	**Where does it take place?**
What happened? **or** **What was the problem?**	**How does it end?**

Reproducible

Fill in the Blanks

The story below is missing some words. Help the writer by filling in the blanks. The word under each line tells you which type of word to use.

The night was dark and _____ . The wind was _____ ,
                              (adjective)   (verb)

and the _____ were _____ . Two little
            (plural noun)   (verb)

_____ were walking through the woods. They _____
   (plural noun)   (verb)

beside a tree and began to _____ . Suddenly, a
                                  (verb)

_____ jumped in front of them. It had two _____ ears
      (noun)   (adjective)

and a _____ nose. It let go a _____ cry. It's teeth
          (adjective)   (adjective)

looked like _____ . The two little _____ felt
                (plural noun)   (plural noun)

_____ . Suddenly, they knew who the strange _____
   (adjective)   (noun)

was. It was _____!
               (proper noun)

Activity 12: Something to Talk About

1 Review with children dialogue in the books they read.

2 Speculate with children ideas for things that the book characters might talk about. Topics could be things related to the story or things that all children can understand, such as a favorite sports team, a television program, a book, or even school.

3 Encourage children to write a new exchange of dialogue between the two characters. Tell students to choose a topic for their characters to talk about.

4 As children write, make sure they use quotation marks correctly.

5 Have children exchange papers with partners to read their dialogues together, each taking the role of a story character.

6 Invite volunteers to share their dialogues with the class.

Activity 13: Storybook Interviews

1 Encourage children to think about questions they would like to ask characters in a story. If they could interview them, what would they like to know?

2 Reproduce and pass out the interview sheet on page 121. Have children pretend they are reporters, asking these questions of the character. Challenge them to answer the questions as they imagine the story character might.

3 Invite children who chose the same story character to compare and contrast their interviews.

Activity 14: Real-Life Interviews

1 Have children expand their interviews by interviewing people in real life. Reproduce and pass out the interview sheet on page 122. Go over the questions with the class. Point out that each question is followed by a question mark.

2 Encourage the class to ask these questions of their classmates, the school librarian, the gym teacher, a class aide, or other people in school. Tell children to record their answers with a tape recorder. You might have children work with partners, letting pairs participate in the interviews over a few days.

3 Back in class, have children listen to the tapes and write down the answers in sentence form to practice their writing skills.

Storybook Interviews

Choose a character from a story that interests you. Think about the character's personality. Pretend that you are interviewing the character. How would the character answer? Write the character's answers on the lines next to each question.

Character's Name: _____

From the Book: _____

What is something important that happened in your life?

_____

_____

Who is your favorite person? Why?

_____

_____

If you could do one thing over, what would it be?

_____

_____

What advice would you give to someone my age?

_____

_____

Real-Life Interviews

Think about someone in school that you would like to interview.
It could be the librarian, a cafeteria worker, a teacher, even someone
in your class. Ask the questions below to find out more about this person.
Write the answers on the lines.

1. What is your favorite color? _____

2. What is your favorite food? _____

3. What is your favorite holiday? _____

4. What is your favorite season? _____

   Why? _____

5. What is your favorite book? _____

   What do you like about it? _____

6. What is your favorite sport? _____

   Can you play the sport? _____

7. What is your favorite movie? _____

   What do you like about it? _____

8. What is your favorite animal? _____

   Why? _____

9. What hobbies do you have? _____

10. If you could go anywhere in the world, where would you go? _____

    Why? _____

Reproducible

Activity 15: Journal Entries

1 Suggest to children that a character in a story they are reading keeps a journal. What might the character write about the things that happened in the story? Brainstorm some ideas with the class.

2 Invite children to write their own journal entries for the story character. To get in the mood, suggest that they start their writings with the salutation *Dear Journal*. Have children consider how the character feels, adding words to describe emotions and actions.

3 After reviewing children's work, suggest that they keep journals themselves, jotting down anecdotes about their day. You might set aside a short time toward the end of each day for this task.

Activity 16: Write a Letter

1 Encourage children to write letters based on their story characters in two ways. First, pass out stationary, or let children create their own stationary on which to write.

2 Suggest that the story character wishes to write a letter to a friend in another town about the events that happened in the story. Encourage children to write such a letter from the character's point of view.

3 Or, invite children to write a letter to the character. Suggest that they ask questions, sympathize, or share something about their own lives.

4 Pass out envelopes, and ask children to address them with places from the story or with made-up names and addresses for friends of the book character.

5 Have the students "mail" the letters to each other, sharing their work with classmates.

Activity 17: Name the Story

1 Ahead of time, choose four books that the class particularly enjoys. Select one passage from each book that children will respond to. Read these passages into a tape recorder.

2 Display the books in your reading center, along with the tape recorder. Provide headphones, if necessary.

3 Invite children to listen to the first selection on the tape. Challenge them to figure out which book it is from.

4 Have them continue to listen to the recordings, matching the passages with the books.

5 To extend this listening activity into a writing activity, invite children to choose one passage that they especially like. Encourage them to write a paragraph about the book using words from this passage.

Activity 18: Radio Dramas

1 Invite children to have fun with a story they read by turning it into a radio drama. Ask children to select a scene from a book they enjoyed.

2 Working in groups, have students divide the tasks. For example, one student could read the narrator's words, several students could read the dialogue, and another student could provide sound effects.

3 Set aside time for children to rehearse their radio dramas. As they read their stories, encourage them to notice parts of speech, punctuation, types of words, similes, metaphors, and other figurative language the author used.

4 Supply children with tape recorders, and invite them to record their radio dramas.

5 Each day, play another group's recordings. You might share with children that before television was invented, people listened to entertainment programs in this way. Invite children to share their thoughts about the experience.

Activity 19: Character Comparison

1 Invite children to compare characters in a book they read by completing a Venn diagram. Reproduce the Venn diagram on page 127 for children to complete on their own. Also draw the diagram on the chalkboard, as shown below, to review with students.

2 Write one character's name above the first circle, and the second character's name above the second circle.

3 Tell children to record what makes the character special in each circle. Use the space in the center to write things the characters have in common.

4 Encourage children to use Venn diagrams to compare story elements as well.

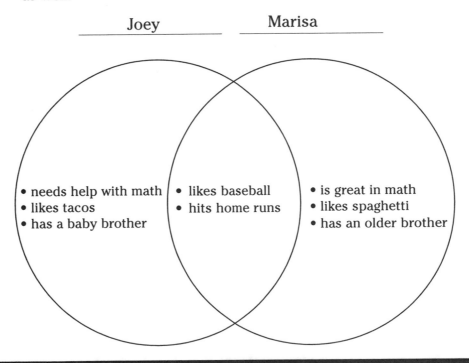

Joey   Marisa

- needs help with math
- likes tacos
- has a baby brother

- likes baseball
- hits home runs

- is great in math
- likes spaghetti
- has an older brother

Activity 20: Put It All Together

1 Now that children have explored parts of speech, types of words, sentence structure, and punctuation, encourage the class to write its own story. Show the class several pictures. They can be book covers, pictures from magazines, or pictures taken from nonfiction texts. Ask the class to vote on the picture they like best.

2 Explain to children that they are going to use the picture to write a story. Start them off with a story starter related to the picture. Write the sentence on chart paper.

3 Going around the room, invite each student to offer one sentence for the class story. Remind them that the sentence should follow the story sequence. Encourage them to use descriptive words and help you correctly punctuate the sentences as you write them down.

4 Read the story back to the class. Let children make any changes.

5 To further practice their writing skills, ask children to copy the class story to take home and share with their families.

Character Comparisons

Choose two characters from a book you are reading. Compare the characters by completing this Venn diagram. Follow the directions at the bottom of the page.

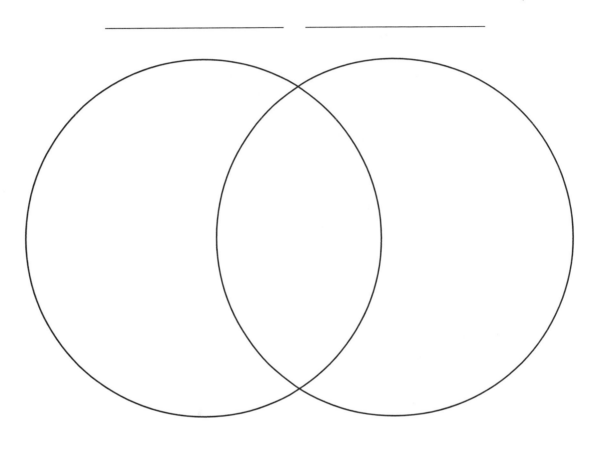

Book Title: _____

Author: _____

1. Write the character's name on the lines above the diagram.

2. In the circle under each character, write descriptive words that tell about the character. What makes him or her special or unique?

3. In the center section, write words that explain what the characters have in common.

4. Write the book title and author on the line below the diagram.

Culminating Activities

Children always need to practice language skills, whether it be recognizing a verb from a noun, forming a question, or noticing how some words sound the same but have different meanings. But class time, as you know, is limited. These remaining culminating activities require little or no advance planning, props, or organization. They encourage children to focus language learning. They can be started quickly, engaged in for a short period of time, and ended abruptly. They can also be adapted to just about any learning level. And most of all, they provide children with quick, simple ways to practice language skills.

Activity 1: Pass the Ball

1 Arrange children in a circle. Select an item to be passed from student to student, such as a ball or a beanbag.

2 Then pose a question for students to ask each other as they pass the ball. Start them off by saying, "My name is _____ . What's your name?" Pass the ball to the child on your right.

3 Invite the child to repeat the sentence and question: "My name is Jim. What's your name?" The child turns to his right, passing along the ball.

4 When the ball comes back to you, ask children another question, such as "My favorite color is red. What is your favorite color?"

5 Continue asking questions and passing the ball as interest holds. Other questions you could ask include: "What's your favorite food?" "What's your favorite story character?" "In which month were you born?" and so on.

Activity 2: Letter Relay

1 Divide the class into two teams.

2 Explain that you are going to present team members with a letter. They are to think of a word that begins with that letter, write the word as quickly as possible, then give the paper to the next child.

3 The second student reads the word, writes another word that starts with the same letter, then passes the paper to the next teammate.

4 Instruct children to keep passing the paper and writing words that start with the same letter. Make sure children review the words their teammates have written before them so they don't write the same word twice.

5 The team who finishes first is the winner. Make sure you review children's words to be sure they are spelled correctly and that none have been duplicated.

Activity 3: Create a Character

1 Ask the class to help you create a character for a story you would like to write.

2 On chart paper, write sentences for children to complete that help explain the character's personality, such as:

- My name is _____ .
- I am _____ years old.
- I live in _____ .
- My favorite food is _____ .
- I have a pet _____ . Its name is _____ .
- I really like to _____ .
- My mother works at _____ .
- My father works at _____ .

3 Encourage children to use descriptive words in their answers.

4 When time allows, incorporate children's character into a class story.

Activity 4: Alphabet Soup

1 Place letter cards in a bowl.

2 Divide the class into teams.

3 Pick a letter from the bowl.

4 Provide children with a time limit, then challenge them to work together to write down as many words as possible that start with that letter.

5 Review children's words.

6 The team with the most correct words gets five points, the next team gets four points, and so on. Continue play as interest holds.

7 At the end of the game, add up the teams' points. The team with the highest score wins.

Activity 5: Syllable Dice Throw

1 Divide the class into teams. Write team names on the chalkboard.

2 Invite one member from each team to the board. Then roll a die.

3 Challenge team members to write a word with the number of syllables shown on the die.

4 Review all the words with the class to determine if they are correct.

Activity 6: Word Association

1 Choose important words from a story the class is reading.

2 Present each word to the class, and invite children to say the first words that pop into their heads that relate to the story. Have older children write their words, then share them aloud.

3 You could also try this as a one-on-one activity for children who need a bit more instructional attention.

Activity 7: Alphabet Roundup

1 Arrange the class in a circle. Sit in the circle, too, holding a box of letter cards.

2 Pick a card from the box, and say a word that starts with that letter.

3 Pass the card to the child on your right, and challenge him or her to provide another word that starts with that letter.

4 Write children's words on chart paper so no words are duplicated.

5 When the card comes back to you, choose another letter and begin again.

Activity 8: Lightbulb Vocabulary

1 Ahead of time, cut out lightbulb shapes. In each lightbulb, write a word from a story the class is reading that you would like to review. Rank the words by difficulty: 50 watt, 75 watt, and 100 watt.

2 Working with small groups, invite children to choose a word, define it, and use it in a sentence. Keep score by adding up the wattage of each bulb.

3 When you feel children have had enough vocabulary practice, add up the wattage. The student with the most points is the winner.

Activity 9: Category Count

1 Present the class with a category such as ocean animals, sports you play with balls, insects, flowers, books by a favorite author.

2 Instruct children to work in groups and write down as many items for the category as they can in two minutes.

3 Tell children when to start and stop.

4 Review children's words to make sure they fit the category. Then count them up. The team with the most correct items is the winner.

Activity 10: Secret in a Box

1 Place an object in a box that represents something in a story you are reading with the class.

2 Allow children to shake the box to determine what the object is. Have them consider the object's weight, the sound it makes, and its possible size. Remind children that the object has to do with the story they are reading.

3 Invite children to brainstorm ideas as you write them on the chalkboard.

4 Reveal the item to confirm their guesses.

Activity 11: More Picture Fun

1 This is another way to hone children's visual discrimination, memory, and critical thinking skills using an illustration from the book. Invite children to study an illustration, for about 30 seconds to a minute.

2 Cover up the picture.

3 Ask children specific questions about the picture to recall details. For example, you might ask the color of clothing people are wearing or the placement of objects to review prepositions. Also ask children to describe any actions taking place. The illustration itself will present questions for you to ask.

4 Record children's responses on chart paper. Then reveal the photo to check their answers.

Activity 12: Hot Rocks

1 This simple game reinforces children's use and understanding of the pronouns *her* and *him*. Seat the class in a circle.

2 Give a ball or beanbag to one child. Tell the child to imagine that it is a hot rock. Ask the child to quickly pass the rock to the person on his or her right as he or she says, "I pass it to him," or "I pass it to her."

3 Each child in turn passes the "hot rock" as quickly as possible, reciting the line as appropriate.

4 An alternate sentence for children to try is, "It's hers!" or "It's his!"

Activity 13: Quick Look

1 To hone letter recognition and visual discrimination skills, invite the class to sit in a circle. Pass out a magazine, mail-order catalog, or newspaper to each child.

2 Invite children to flip through their periodicals to get a quick look at what's inside.

3 After about a minute, tell children to stop, and encourage them to share with the group the things they saw in their magazines. If possible, try to focus the discussion on articles related to a book the class is currently reading. Pose such questions as, "Did anyone see a picture of or a word for the animal we are reading about?" "Did anyone see a picture that looks like the setting of the book?"

4 Conclude by comparing with children how magazines and newspapers differ from books.

Activity 14: Magazine Pictures

1 At random, show children pictures from magazines. Invite children to describe the images they see in the pictures. Encourage them to identify colors and shapes, and use prepositions to point out where things are.

2 Tell children that this picture is part of an article. Speculate what the article might be about. Write down children's ideas.

3 Then show children the title of the article and help them read it.

4 You might make this a team game, scoring points for each correct guess.

Activity 15: Make a Magazine

1 Provide children with magazines they can cut up.

2 Invite children to choose an article they particularly like and cut it out.

3 Have children glue the article to a sheet of paper. Make sure all students are using the same-size paper.

4 Combine children's papers into a class magazine. Keep the magazine in your reading center, encouraging children to read it.

Activity 16: Grab-Bag Descriptions

1 Place a small object in a bag. If possible, choose an object that relates to a book the class is reading.

2 Invite a child to reach into the bag to feel it. Encourage the student to describe for the class what he or she feels. For example, is the object smooth or rough or fuzzy? Does it have corners? Can they feel a particular shape?

3 As the student describes the object, ask the rest of the class to figure out what the object could be. Jot down their ideas on the chalkboard.

4 Remove the item from the bag to confirm their answers. If applicable, talk with children about how the item relates to the book.

5 Invite another student to describe another mystery object. Continue as interest holds.

Activity 17: Odd-Ball Object

1 Place a group of objects on a table that all the children can see (for example, a pencil, crayon, marker, paintbrush, and pad of paper).

2 Invite children to study the items. Explain that four of the objects have something in common, and therefore, form a group. But one object is the odd ball—it doesn't belong.

3 Challenge children to not only figure out which is the odd-ball object, but also determine the criteria for the group. (In the example, the criteria is things we write with. The paper is the odd-ball object.)

4 After you've presented several items to the class, encourage children to come up with their own groupings, matching like objects and naming one as the odd ball.

Activity 18: The Complete Picture

1 Show children an illustration from a book the class is about to read. However, cover up half of the illustration.

2 Encourage children to describe what they think the other half of the picture looks like. What images will they see? What colors? What animals or plants? What shapes?

3 Reveal the entire illustration to confirm their ideas.

Activity 19: What's Missing?

1 Go through a magazine, and cover up an object in a picture with a self-stick note.

2 Show the picture to the class. Challenge children to tell you what is missing. What is under the paper?

3 Invite children to describe the missing object as you write down their ideas.

4 Then remove the note to fully reveal the picture.

5 If you wish, you can make this a team game, giving children points for each correct answer.

Activity 20: Look at a Book

1 As a prereading exercise, show children an illustration from a book they are about to read. The picture could also be the cover, but make sure you cover up the title.

2 Invite children to describe the picture. Who do they think the people or animals are? What are they doing? How are they feeling? What clues does the illustration provide?

3 Explain to children that this picture is from a book they are about to read. Speculate what the book might be about. Write down children's ideas.

4 Then show children the title of the book and share the basic plot. Review children's predictions to see which were closest.

5 Now open your book and begin to read.

APPENDIX

9-Square Bingo Game Board

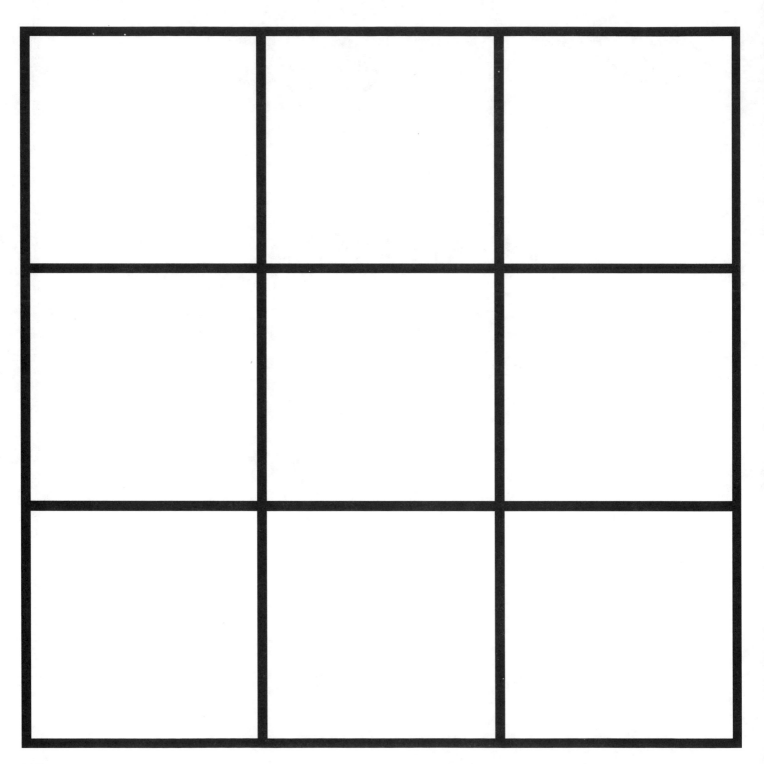

Reproducible

16-Square Bingo Game Board

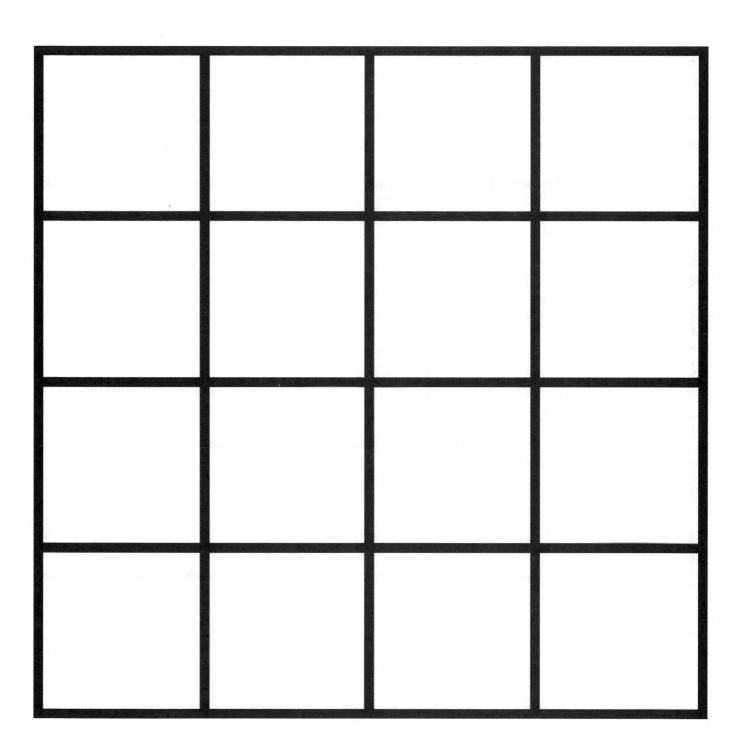

25-Square Bingo Game Board

		FREE		

Reproducible © Fearon Teacher Aids FE7961

Puzzle Patterns

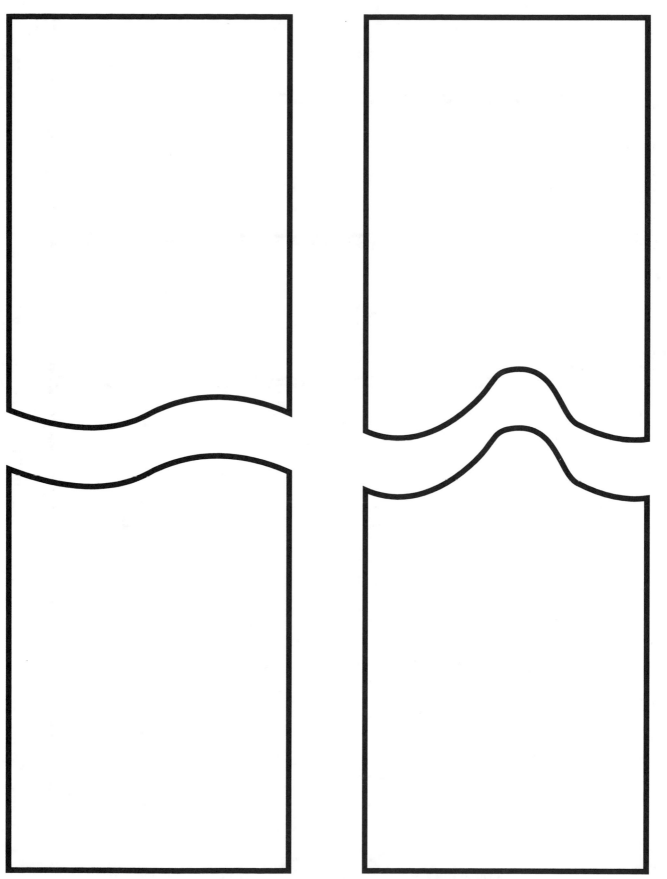

Reproducible

Cluster Chart

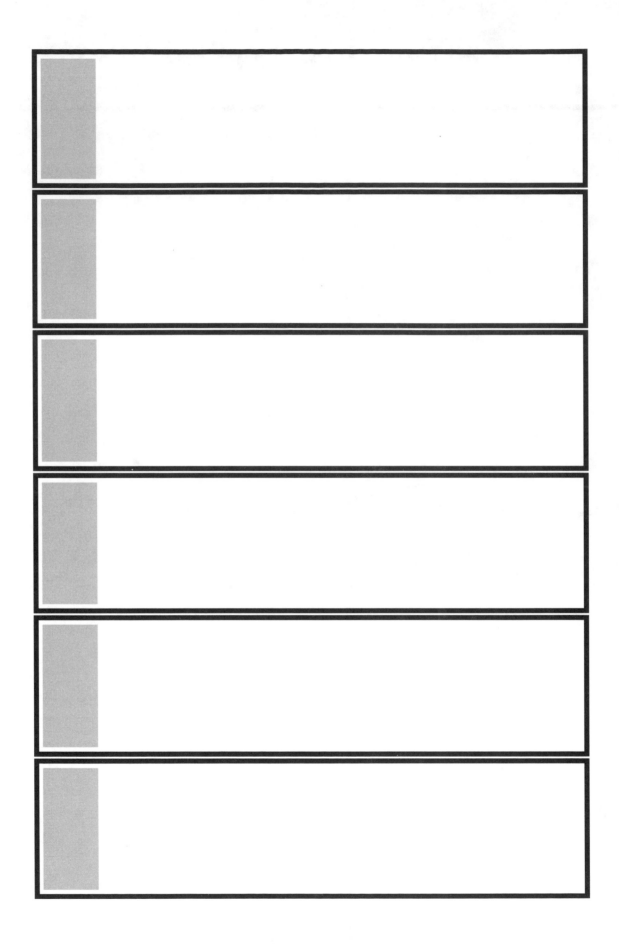

Reproducible

Clock Pattern

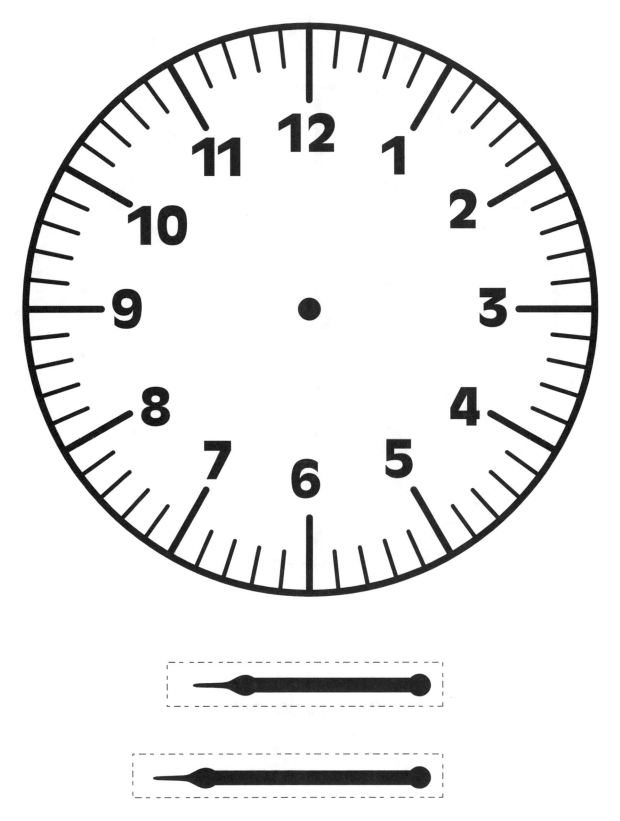

Reproducible 143

Spinner Pattern

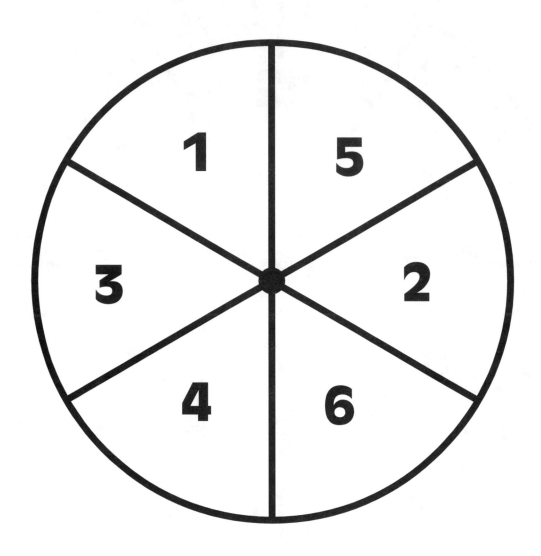

Reproducible